"*Rock-a My Soul* is a most engaging handbook for all whose faith is intertwined with popular music. In friendly prose for seekers of all kinds, David Nantais shows that concert halls and music collections are the postmodern mangers where new and enduring spiritual identities are being born. And to this scene of new birth he comes bearing guitars, drums, bass—and a vivid appreciation for the importance of mystery and mystical experience. An impassioned traveling companion!"

> — Tom Beaudoin
> Associate Professor of Theology
> Fordham University

"A tension between the worldly and the spiritual has existed in rock 'n' roll since its foundations in African-American spirituals, gospel, and blues music. But for Catholic drummer Nantais, the very music often feared by religious folk has served as both balm and outlet to help him understand God. In this short, first-person musing, Nantais argues that 'theology can be done through music,' encouraging Christians to see rock 'n' roll as a 'mode of theological expression.' Setting aside contemporary Christian music (which he says is not the only way to marry rock and religion), he argues that mainstream rock has many virtues: community building and transcendent elements, meditative qualities, expression of emotion. Nantais admits to some less edifying aspects of rock (e.g., segregated crowds at rock music venues, ties to consumerism). He also chooses not to address a major sticking point for some—offensive lyrics—and so may not be able to convince every reader of rock's merits. Despite that, his enthusiasm for mix tapes and chord progressions is infectious. Christians will learn to find God in a rock concert, and lovers of all things drum and guitar will find spiritual validation."

> — *Publishers Weekly*

"David Nantais is, hands down, one of the best young writers on Christian spirituality: inviting, inventive, and insightful. In *Rock-a My Soul*, he offers a fascinating look at how rock music, often thought to be a threat to faith, can actually support and nourish one's spiritual life. If you're a music fan, Nantais, a rock musician himself, will show you how the music you love can draw you closer to God. If you're a believer, Nantais will serve as an experienced guide to modes of experiencing God that you might never have considered. And if you're a music fan and a believer, well, then this book will, as the band said, rock you."

— James Martin, SJ
Author of *The Jesuit Guide to (Almost) Everything*

ROCK-A MY SOUL

An Invitation to Rock Your Religion

David Nantais

LITURGICAL PRESS

Collegeville, Minnesota

www.litpress.org

© 2011 by David Nantais.

Cover design by Ann Blattner.
Interior design by Mark Warzecha.
Photos courtesy of Photos.com.

Published by Liturgical Press
Saint John's Abbey
PO Box 7500
Collegeville, Minnesota 56321-7500

1   2   3   4   5   6   7   8   9

Library of Congress Cataloging-in-Publication Data

Nantais, David.
   Rock-a my soul : an invitation to rock your religion / David Nantais.
       p.   cm.
    ISBN 978-0-8146-3354-0 (pbk.) —
    ISBN 978-0-8146-3945-0 (e-book)
    1. Rock music—Religious aspects—Christianity.   I. Title.

ML3918.R63N36 2011
261.5'78—dc22

                                                    2010042460

To my wife, Carrie, and son, Liam.

CONTENTS

Acknowledgments

A rock album is a project that can only be realized through the work of several people: musicians, a producer, engineers, managers, and technicians, among others. Likewise, religious ritual often relies on pastors, lay ministers, congregations, and liturgists to come to life. This book, too, would never have been born without the inspiration and encouragement from a host of companions, friends, family members, and bandmates.

My formation as a rock drummer has relied heavily upon the musicians I have been blessed to work with over the past two decades. I am grateful to Joe Leonard; Bryon Dudley; Brian Christopher, SJ; Tom Beaudoin; Tom Christy; and Paul Tiseo for their friendship and for pushing me to be better than I thought I could be. My musical inspiration has come from several sources, but I need to mention Neil Peart, Liberty DeVitto, and Jerry Gaskill as the patron saints of my drumming life.

My formation as a writer has also depended upon the gentle support of many. Thank you, Ed Schmidt, SJ; James

Martin, SJ; Jeremy Langford; and John Predmore, SJ, for your friendship and for seeing potential in my work that was, at times, hidden from me.

Those responsible for my spiritual and religious formation are legion, but a few stand out. My parents John and Roni, the Society of Jesus, and my wife Carrie have all provided signposts at various points in my life that have kept me moving along the path of faith.

While a number of ideas in this book have been rolling around in my head and heart for years, an enriching and rocking weekend at Saint John's in Collegeville, Minnesota, in October of 2007, made possible by Hans Christoffersen and Peter Dwyer, finally gave me the confidence to set these musings to paper.

Thank you to Dan Hill and Carrie Nantais for reading early drafts of this book and providing valuable feedback.

Thank you to Fr. Lyle Wilgenbusch for his help with the title of this book.

Finally, to my "listening room" companions, Dan Hill, Jim Finucan, and Brian Bell. Few things are as consoling as sharing music, laughter, and good food and drink with dear friends. I look forward to becoming "those guys" who, in old age, complain about how contemporary music is not as good as the classic stuff from our youth!

David Nantais
Detroit, Michigan
August 2010

INTRODUCTION

For over five decades, it has been labeled "the Devil's music" and has been
accused of corrupting children. But rock
and roll music emerged from religious
music and, I contend, still maintains
close ties with religion and spirituality
up to the present day. It has also served
as a conduit to spiritual experiences for
its fans and acted as an important aspect
of their life stories. Rock music deserves a serious theological analysis in order for us to appreciate its role in the
spiritual and religious lives of hundreds of thousands of
people. I hope to contribute to the dialogue between rock
music and religion, and help others understand the significance of this relationship. First, though, I will need to
clarify some concepts and terminology in order to help the
reader understand what this project is about and why I
believe it is important.

To begin, the question will inevitably arise, what exactly
is rock music? This question has become more difficult to

answer, and I for one do not believe there is an ideal response. So many different types of music now fall under the "rock music" umbrella, and new subgenres are being developed all the time. While it seems a bit cliché, some have suggested that rock and roll is a lifestyle or a worldview rather than a specific category of music. Rock expresses freedom from oppressive social mores. When society dictates that men should wear their hair short or women should act like "ladies," the rock and roll ethos resists by encouraging long hair, earrings, and the expression of primal emotions. This is a contemporary expression of a rock and roll ideology, but it is grounded in the history of this music. "The first African captives sold into slavery in the New World in the early 1600s carried with them an agonized inspiration that would become the cornerstone for virtually every American music expression to follow."[1] Rock and roll is a child of the black spirituals, songs that were drawn from the horrible experiences of suffering, oppression, and pain endured in slavery. This history, which I will touch upon in chapter 1, is very important for understanding and interpreting rock and roll music.

There may be some confusion regarding what I am trying to accomplish with this project. Is this a theology of rock music? Is this a spirituality of rock music? Is this a Catholic Christian looking at the complex culture of rock music through a religious lens and describing what he sees?

---

[1] Davin Seay with Mary Neely, *Stairway to Heaven: The Spiritual Roots of Rock 'N' Roll* (New York: Ballantine Books, 1986), 15.

My answer to these questions is "Yes!" But I hope that in the end, the whole is greater than the sum of its parts. I have written several articles for primarily religious publications attempting to present religious interpretations of the world of popular culture, which includes rock music, to those who have difficulty seeing anything good in it. I present six of these pieces in chapter 5. Since these projects were expressions of my religious interpretations, they inevitably held some of my own personal bias. This will be true of this book as well. I am expressing my own religious and spiritual views about rock and roll music, which will be different than others' views.

Rock fans know that the music they enjoy is also an avenue to special memories, experiences, and imaginations that are uniquely their own. I am no different in this regard. At the same time, however, I hope that by drawing on a variety of sources, perspectives, and critiques, I am able to provide a general method for those who are fans of rock and roll music to see the spiritual and religious qualities in the music they enjoy. I also hope that this project helps those who are not rock fans, but sit on the periphery as casual observers, to understand a bit more about rock music and how it carries a variety of meanings beyond the music. I do *not* intend this book to be a vehicle for rock proselytizing—in other words, I will not attempt to convince the reader that the rock and roll musicians and bands that I like are the best. I will be using examples drawn from the music I love, but this is just to help readers understand specific points I am attempting to make.

While I do address the topic of "Christian rock" throughout (especially in chapters 1 and 3), this subgenre of rock music is not the focal point of this book. I have disclosed my views about Christian rock previously,[2] and I will explore some of the theological implications of this music further, but I am trying to approach the topic of rock music and religion from a different perspective that is informed by my Catholic background. While there certainly are Catholic bands that fall under the Christian rock umbrella, this music emerged from a distinctly Evangelical Protestant tradition and has retained this cast about it up to the present day. I do not wish to trash Christian rock, but in my attempt to promote a different view of how rock music and religious practice can be integrated, I do present critiques of the theological assumptions that *propel* Christian rock. Ever in front of me is the challenge to help illuminate what theologian and musician Jeremy Begbie believes is sorely lacking in the area of religion and music: "Simply put: music is being grounded firmly in a universal God-given order, and thus it is seen as a means through which we are enabled to live more fully in the world that God has made and with the God who made it."[3]

Next, this project is not comprised of analyses of rock music lyrics. This is a perspective that, I believe, has been

[2] David Nantais, "What Would Jesus Listen To?" *America* (May 21, 2007): 22–24.

[3] Jeremy Begbie, *Resounding Truth: Christian Wisdom in the World of Music* (Grand Rapids: Baker Academic, 2007), 94.

overdone, and while it serves a purpose, it is not the direction in which I wish to go. Lyrical content is an important ingredient in rock music for a variety of reasons, and deserves some attention. For much of its history, however, when rock music has been lambasted for corrupting children, the focus is primarily on scandalous lyrics. Judging music based on a superficial interpretation of lyrics is, I believe, much too simplistic and loses any sense of irony, symbolism, and poetic license that the writer is attempting to utilize. "Songs that mention 'Jesus' are good, but lyrics about sex are bad." This all-too-common perspective, without any grounding in context, does not appreciate the complexity of themes and concepts that a lot of rock music addresses, and does so oftentimes in a very sophisticated way.

In his 1993 book *Running with the Devil: Power, Gender and Madness in Heavy Metal Music*, Robert Walser deftly explains the problems associated with deriving an "objective" meaning for song lyrics. He posits that sociologists who tried studying heavy metal music but were not "insiders," meaning they were not fans of the music they analyzed, often attempted a simplistic popular culture analysis. They made the mistake of reducing the meaning of music to the lyrics, ironically neglecting the music itself, and then assumed a literal interpretation of the lyrics. "This is called 'content' analysis, and it assumes that an outside reader will interpret lyrics just as an insider would; it also assumes a linear communication model, where artists encode meanings that are transmitted to listeners, who then decipher them, rather than a dialectical environment in which meanings are multiple, fluid, and negotiated."[4] After almost three decades of rock fandom and a lifetime as a Christian, I believe that I am enough of an insider to posit a viable perspective about rock and its ties to religion and spiritual practices.

While it may be beyond the scope of this project, I am also intrigued by how theology can be done *through* music. In other words, it is possible that there are characteristics of music that can enable a theologian to alter her perspective and comprehend religious doctrines in a different way, or to apply musical ways of arrangement to theological notions. For an example, I turn to Jeremy Begbie, upon whom I rely for help several times in this book. Begbie recalled a story about the great scholar of the New Testament, N. T. Wright, who worked with a composer named Paul Spicer to create a piece of music for an Easter festival. Once he heard the completed piece of music, Wright, one who has devoted his professional life to studying the New Testament, discovered that he was able to derive more meaning from the resurrection narrative in the Gospel of John than he ever had previously. Begbie quotes an astounded Wright: "My reading, translation of and meditation on Scripture had not shown me all that I now think I

---

[4] Robert Walser, *Running with the Devil: Power, Gender and Madness in Heavy Metal Music* (Middletown: Wesleyan University Press, 1993), 21.

see there."[5] Something within the music that Spicer wrote awakened a new perspective within Wright, or provided a new lens through which he could view John's gospel. This possibility for music to inform theology is an academic project beyond the purpose of this book, but it is something in which I am very interested and would like to mention in the hope of sparking discussions between readers, musicians, and theologians.

As I discussed previously, one cannot discuss rock and roll music without addressing issues of race, especially when elucidating the history of this genre as a derivative of black spirituals and the blues. I attempt to do this in chapter 1 and delve further into issues of race and rock music in chapter 4 under the theme of social justice. Why is it that contemporary rock music is primarily made by and marketed to a white audience? The roots of rock and roll are firmly grounded in the African American community. There is a long history up to the present day of this community not only contributing to rock music but also breaking new ground and revolutionizing it.

The advent of music television, especially MTV and VH1, and the use of rock and roll in blockbuster movies has changed how we listen to this music. Additionally, over the past couple of decades some well-known rock songs are used in commercials to market products to a particular constituency. This integration of rock with

[5] Jeremy Begbie, "The Theological Potential of Music," *Christian Scholar's Review* 33:1 (Fall 2003): 139.

images and products influences not only how we "hear" music in the present but it also has an effect on the memories of music that we love. Psychiatrist and popular author Oliver Sacks, a self-proclaimed atheist, admits that when he sees a menorah in December, old Hanukkah songs play in his mind.[6] There is an emotional connection between the visual and the audio—what we hear and see are often difficult to separate. This phenomenon could be harmless or it could be used by a wily ad agency to manipulate me into purchasing certain products. In chapter 4 on rock music and social justice, I raise this issue and also discuss some of the effects it has on a rock fan's personal identity.

I have been a fan of rock music since I was a young child. I remember listening to Detroit radio in 1981 and hearing The Romantics' song "What I Like About You" charge at me through the speakers like a bull in Pamplona, pushing my primitive radio/cassette player to its limits. I found the experience simultaneously exciting and dangerous. I recall being extremely self-conscious after the song had concluded as I realized that I had shouted out "Hey, Uh-huh" at the chorus with the lead singer. These lyrics were complete gibberish, but they made so much sense to me. They were shouts of release and freedom, and while I could not at that time appreciate the sexual tension communicated in that song, it felt good to shout, to give voice to whatever nascent angst I harbored in my young

---

[6] Oliver Sacks, *Musicophilia: Tales of Music and the Brain* (New York: Alfred A. Knopf, 2007), 35.

soul. I wondered if anyone in the house had heard me, and whether I would get in trouble for engaging in such pagan revelry. This was, after all, not church music. But it was definitely spiritual music, and the experience of listening to rock music on that day and since has changed my life. In chapter 6, I share my spiritual/musical autobiography and elaborate more on how rock music has been a spiritual exercise for me.

Finally, I would be remiss if I did not acknowledge the importance of the spirituality of St. Ignatius Loyola for help in writing this book. As a former Jesuit, my life is still very much informed by the *Spiritual Exercises*, as is obvious from the numerous times I utilize their wisdom in this book. Ignatius's "mission statement" can be found in his "Principle and Foundation":

> Human beings are created to praise, reverence, and serve God our Lord, and by means of doing this to save their souls. The other things on the face of the earth are created for the human beings, to help them in the pursuit of the end for which they are created.[7]

Simply put, rock and roll music is part of God's creation. It is a gift that, I believe, can be used in spiritual and religious contexts, and can help people praise, reverence, and serve God. For those who continue reading this book, I hope you

[7] George E. Ganss, SJ, *The Spiritual Exercises of Saint Ignatius* (St. Louis: Institute of Jesuit Sources, 1992), 32.

find it intellectually stimulating and that it encourages you to examine the music you love and to seek God there.

Long Live Rock!
A.M.D.G.

Chapter 1

ROCK AND ROLL'S "PAGAN SPIRITS"*

On the evening of June 5, 1956, a young and upcoming rock and roll singer named Elvis Presley appeared on the Milton Berle show. Teenagers loved watching him perform on television, but parents and culture commentators were less than thrilled. It was not so much Elvis's singing that bothered them as it was the style in which he performed. While singing, he gyrated his hips in a suggestive and sexual manner. In their June 23, 1956, issue of the Catholic magazine *America*, the Jesuit priest editors did not contain their outright disgust for Elvis, his music, and his controversial live performance. "If his 'entertainment' could be confined to records," they opined, "it might not be too bad

* Parts of this chapter first appeared in David Nantais, "What Would Jesus Listen To?" *America* (May 21, 2007): 22–24.

an influence on the young, but unfortunately Presley makes personal appearances."[1] The priest writers went on to quote negative reviews of Mr. Presley's television appearance from the *San Francisco Chronicle* and the *New York Times*. But it was the sons of St. Ignatius who struck the most wrenching blow with this closing statement: "If the agencies (TV and other) would stop handling such nauseating stuff, all the Presleys of our land would soon be swallowed up in the oblivion they deserve."[2] This incident was not the last time that religion clashed with rock and roll.

It seems that music and Christianity have had a tense relationship since immediately after Jesus walked out of the tomb. By the time rock and roll music burst onto the scene, Christianity already had a long and rigid tradition of condemning various types of music for over nineteen centuries. In the second century BCE, Christians were suspicious of music because of its associations with pagan worship rites. At that time and since, music was also thought to be dangerously appealing to the flesh and the "lower passions," thus neglecting the sanctity of the human spirit.[3] The desire to dichotomize spirit and flesh has been a strong motivating force working to suppress music and its potential power. While the reasons for condemnation

[1] The editors of *America* magazine, "Beware Elvis Presley" in "Current Comment" (June 23, 1956): 294.

[2] Ibid., 295.

[3] Richard Viladesau, *Theology and the Arts: Encountering God through Music, Art and Rhetoric* (New York: Paulist Press, 2000), 15.

change over the centuries, at the core of them all seems to be fear—fear of music's power, fear of sexuality/flesh, and fear of "the other," especially African Americans.

Why would music cause people to fear? In this chapter, I would like to explore some of the reasons why Christianity feared to embrace various types of music for so long, even to the present day. Theologians Tom Beaudoin and Brian Robinette, writing in an article in *America* magazine about rock music, point out that "too much Christian writing on the subject has been negative and antagonistic, focusing more on sensational lyrics than on its religiously meaningful effects."[4] My hope is to add a fresh voice to the dialogue about rock music and religion, and that my perspective will be a catalyst for further thought and discussion. To this end, I will examine some of the religious roots of rock and roll music and how its early practitioners tried to navigate their way through the inevitable tensions that arose between Christianity and rock music. Finally, I examine the phenomenon of Christian rock music, which has attempted to serve as a bridge or negotiator between rock music and Christianity. While its efforts are somewhat commendable, I conclude the chapter by suggesting that there are other ways to bring these two immense cultural forces to the table and perhaps even negotiate a peaceful harmony.

[4] Tom Beaudoin and Brian Robinette, "Stairway to Heaven: Can You be Saved by Rock 'n' Roll?" *America* 201, no. 11 (October 26, 2009): 19.

Early Christian Views on Music

The great philosopher Plato was obviously not a Christian, as he was born over four centuries before Jesus walked the earth. But his work has had an enormous impact on Christianity, especially through its influence on St. Augustine and St. Thomas Aquinas. Plato actually wrote about music, but his perspective is hardly straightforward. He praises music for its potential to bring human beings' souls into harmony with one another. According to Jeremy Begbie, "In this way, music and morality become closely linked. According to the ancient Greek conception of 'ethos,' music, through its direct influence on the harmony of the soul, can influence the formation of good character."[5] Plato's understanding of the human person, while he did not have the benefit of modern psychological science, does resonate in some important ways. He viewed music as a means for positive social behavior, community building, and bringing harmony to the *polis*, or the city. Music certainly can and has provided a means for bringing people together with common tastes to share their enjoyment with one another. It would be nice to think that music could also help one develop virtuous behavior. The influence of music on human behavior is a controversial subject. While it holds no facile answers, it is an issue to which I give attention throughout the book.

---

[5] Jeremy Begbie, *Resounding Truth: Christian Wisdom in the World of Music* (Grand Rapids: Baker Academic, 2007), 80.

Plato could also be critical of music. Plato was skeptical of material reality. He believed in the "Forms," or that the ideal essence of everything existed in a distinct world. All of the things of the earth only participate in these Forms; we cannot grasp fully what anything is unless we focus on the Form of which it is an imitation. Understanding the Form means understanding the Truth. Music, too, is only good insofar as it participates in its ideal Form. Plato wondered whether music could sometimes lead its listeners astray, further and further away from the ideal and true Form.[6] Plato also believed that while music could encourage harmony of the soul, it could also cause dissonance in the soul if it stirred up strong emotions that moved a person away from reason. He was especially critical of instrumental music in this regard. Lyrics, he believed, could keep a check on the music and direct the listener toward the higher passions.

Plato's critiques of music have had a lasting impact on Christianity for hundreds of years, due in large part to Christian thinkers who were greatly influenced by his philosophy. The dichotomy he set up between the material (world) and the Forms (spiritual) haunts Christianity even today. Suspicion of "worldly pleasures" is a common theme in some Catholic and Protestant circles, and it is cast over music among other sensual experiences. Plato's notion that music can encourage wild, uncivilized behavior has also created a legacy. The horrible massacre in 1999 at

[6] Ibid., 81.

Columbine High School in Littleton, Colorado, left many people stunned and grasping for answers. How could these teenage boys commit such ghastly violence? Among the dozens of suggestions proffered was that the music to which the boys listened, in this case the shock-rock star Marilyn Manson, caused them to become murderers. This is, I believe, an overly simplistic explanation for what is a complex psychological, sociological, and spiritual problem. No one can deny the power of music to spark an emotional response, but complex human actions, I believe, cannot be reduced to simple cause and effect explanations.[7]

Saint Augustine also felt conflicted about music, especially the use of music in Christian liturgy. His mentor, St. Ambrose, had initiated the use of liturgical music in the Milanese church. Augustine was more cautiously reserved about liturgical music. He, like Plato, viewed music with a good dose of skepticism due to its appeal to "the flesh." Theologian Richard Viladesau observes that Augustine "is attracted by the usefulness of song for raising the soul to God, but on the other hand he fears that its pleasures will entrap the soul in a lower order of beauty and prevent its ascent to the true Good."[8] Augustine is genuinely concerned for the human soul. If material reality gets too firm a grip on one's soul, the result could be idolatry—replacing worship of the Creator with worship of creation. Insofar as music can direct the listener's heart to God, it is helpful.

---

[7] David Nantais, "CDs Don't Kill People . . .," *America* 182, no. 1 (January 1, 2000): 14–15.

[8] Viladesau, 18.

But according to Augustine, it is not an art form that should be enjoyed for its own sake.

In *The Confessions*, arguably his most famous work, Augustine admits to experiencing both sides of the tug-of-war between the spirit and flesh. With regard specifically to music, Augustine writes that after he embraced Christianity, he found much consolation in liturgical music but not in the music per se. Rather, it was the words sung and presumably the holy thoughts the words conjured. There were times, Augustine admits, when he found himself enjoying the songs more than their subject. Augustine referred to these episodes as "sins" and added that once he realized the error of his ways, he wished to no longer hear any singing.[9] For Augustine, anything that distracted a person from God could lead one to sin. Music must direct the heart, mind, and soul to God. If this does not happen, the fault is not so much in the music, according to Augustine, but rather in the intention of the listener. Music, then, could at times serve as the near occasion of sin. Augustine did not believe that the material world was evil, as he is sometimes characterized. But the material world for him had a purpose—to direct one to God. "His main concern is with our attitude, the attitude of the soul; we must love things, so to speak, 'toward God,' not for themselves."[10]

As Christianity spread throughout the world from the time of Augustine up through the Middle Ages, the Church embraced liturgical music much more. The memory of

[9] Ibid., 19.
[10] Begbie, 86.

music being associated with pagan rituals faded rapidly, and when Latin became the universal language of Christian liturgy, music served as a way for the majority of the congregation to engage in a religious experience without having to understand the words the priest spoke.[11] It was from this historical backdrop that Thomas Aquinas wrote about music—a much different context than Augustine. Richard Viladesau highlights the primary difference: "First of all, he [Aquinas] rejects the Platonic division between spirit and flesh: Corporeal song can also be spiritual and can lead to spiritual devotion."[12] This is a very important development in Christianity's outlook regarding music. Aquinas did not deny that music could be abused—especially by being "overly theatrical" in a liturgical setting. But he begins with an affirmative stance about the use of music in Christian liturgy. Music focuses the people in the congregation on the power and majesty of the divine. In this regard, it is a useful worship aid and elicits powerful emotions in the listener—feelings of love and transcendence, which help the faithful reduce the gap between human and divine.

Aquinas believed that even if a worshiper in a congregation could not understand the words to a liturgical song, the song would still be fulfilling its purpose due to the intention of those singing it. This, according to Viladesau, is another important distinction between Augustine and Aquinas, which Thomas describes in an article in his

---

[11] Viladesau, 20.
[12] Ibid.

famous *Summa Theologiae*. "Even though Thomas cites Augustine as his authority and quotes him several times in the article, he ends up going far beyond Augustine in saying that singing has a valid place in worship, *even if the words cannot be understood*."[13] If the person or persons singing the song are intending the music to praise God, then it can have a positive effect on the souls of the listeners, presumably since their holy intention would come across in other ways, such as the fervor and joy in their voices.

This is a vital point to which I will return, especially when I discuss the issue of Christian rock music, also called CCM—Contemporary Christian Music. CCM tends to overlook the importance of intention in a song and instead focuses on words as its distinctive trait. There is no way to distinguish a "secular" hard rock song from a Christian hard rock song except for the lyrical content. If intention— the singer's, the band's, the songwriter's—is an important part of what defines a song's purpose and value, as Aquinas posits, then one need not utilize overtly religious lyrics to communicate a message about God.

Many of the early Church reformers, beginning in the sixteenth century, held music at arm's length and distrusted its power. Martin Luther, interestingly, was not one of them. Music was a part of Luther's life from the time he was a child, and continued to be through his tenure in the Augustinian order. He not only enjoyed listening to music but he also sang and played the lute, a popular instrument

---

[13] Ibid., 22.

of the time. It is clear from his writings on music that Luther appreciated music's power to move the soul and to stir up powerful emotions and desires. Luther referred to music as a gift from God. Begbie summarizes Luther's feelings thus: "Music is a means, granted by God, through which we are given to share in and enjoy the basic God-given order of the world."[14] According to Begbie, the sense of order that music embodied was very important to Luther. Just as God created the universe by placing order in the midst of chaos, music also places order in the world by arranging notes and sounds in a certain way. Without order in music, the result would be cacophony.

Luther embraced music and its effect on the human person with a passion not found in any of his Reformer contemporaries, many of whom leaned toward a distrust of anything appealing to the flesh in favor of spiritual perfection. Luther was exceptionally fond of music's ability to evoke emotions. His writing suggests that music is one of the best ways to lift the spirits of the depressed and calm those who are too aggressive.[15] Luther was well aware of Augustine's views on music, especially his wariness about its emotional impact on people. His perspective on music, particularly his strong belief in its giftedness from God, persuaded Luther to stand firm, even in the face of a disagreement with one of the Church fathers. Begbie notes, "Supporting this is a view of the human person noticeably

[14] Begbie, 99.
[15] Ibid., 103.

more integrated than some of his forefathers—with less distrust of the senses and a greater awareness of the goodness of the physical body."[16] Luther's sense of freedom about music is instructive. His personal experiences growing up with music and enjoying it led him to find a way to integrate this passion with his faith. Familiarity, it seems, does not breed contempt when it comes to music.

What can we garner from this brief overview of pre- and early Christian notions about music? First, the flesh/spirit dichotomy that we saw in Plato's work (although hardly exclusive to him) has been a thorn in the side of Christianity since the beginning. The "flesh" and "spirit" have been engaged in a theological tug-of-war that Christianity has refereed for over two millennia, at times allowing one side (usually the spirit) to gain an advantage. Theologians such as Augustine and some of the Reformers who were much more skeptical of music and its power to entice the flesh were not trying to be killjoys, but were, to give them the benefit of the doubt, honestly concerned about the human soul. Anything that wasn't of the spirit, they thought, had the power to corrupt and even destroy the soul. We can see this current running through the history of rock and roll music, which I address in the next section. It will be helpful, I believe, to recognize this flesh/spirit struggle as it is manifest in rock music critiques, and develop a more nuanced approach to deal with it.

[16] Ibid.

One common thread among these four historical figures is that each spoke from experience. Whether they were more skeptical or accepting of music, they heard and appreciated it at some level before passing judgment. This is a vital lesson for us as we approach the history of rock music and the potential spiritual and religious experiences that can come from this genre. Rock music is not above reproach just because there are potential spiritual fruits to be gained from immersing oneself in it. Before critiquing it, however, one needs to listen and listen actively. Part of my desire for writing this book is to help people appreciate rock music in a different way. Some reading this may be casual fans who do not feel strongly one way or the other about rock. Others may be passionate about the music but never considered the spiritual potential in it. Still others may be highly skeptical and even fearful of rock music's effect on children, especially their own. All of these groups, I believe, can gain new insights by listening or relistening to this music from a different vantage point after reflecting on the themes I present. We can then begin a more beneficial conversation on the subject, one not founded upon fear.

Rock and Roll's Religious Pedigree

"The powerful God of Christianity was waging war with the pantheon of pagan spirits. It was in the heat of that battle that rock 'n' roll was forged."[17] This dramatic

---

[17] Davin Seay with Mary Neely, *Stairway to Heaven: The Spiritual Roots of Rock 'N' Roll* (New York: Ballantine Books, 1986), 13.

representation of the birth of rock and roll points to the tense relationship rock music and Christianity have endured for decades. Much of the tension is, to put it simply, because what rock and roll is about to many can seem to be the antithesis of what religion—or in this case, Christianity—is about. Rock promotes freedom, excess, experimentation with sex and drugs, expressing anger at authority, and rebelling from social conventions. Christianity, on the other hand, often promotes obedience to authority—human and divine—relying on tradition for guidance, living for others, and being a responsible contributor to the community. It may surprise many, then, that rock and roll music emerged from religious music and, I argue, still retains the effects of its historical identity at its core. This section will explore the religious roots of rock music and hopefully highlight how these roots helped one of the most popular contemporary genres of music thrive for decades.

Rock and roll's history, tragically, is associated with institutionalized slavery in the United States. As slaves were brought to the United States from Africa starting in the early 1600s, the landowners would often force them to abandon their former religious practice and embrace the "true religion" of Christianity. The plantation owners would often distort Christian teachings to keep the slaves in line, for example, by claiming that it pleased God for slaves to remain obedient to their "masters." The African slaves, having come from a very religious culture, were not strangers to rituals, and would create their own forms of worship that combined their traditional tribal practices with some learned Christian practices. These worship "services" were held whenever the slaves could get out of the owner's sight for an extended period of time. Their form varied, but they always included music.[18] It was at these gatherings that the black spiritual was created. Spirituals are a form of song that cried out for freedom from oppression to the God that liberated Moses and the Israelites, among others.[19] These songs played a significant role in slaves' lives and are still very important to African Americans today.

The spiritual is a revered form of music that also played a significant role in the creation of several other musical forms, including the blues, gospel, and rock and roll. Not surprising, at the heart of the spiritual is the felt experience of God's Holy Spirit. These cannot be separated—the music and the religious experience are one. African American theologian James Cone writes that in order to understand the religious significance of the spirituals, one should not reduce understanding to an academic exercise. Rather, "the interpreter must *feel* the Spirit; that is, one must feel one's way into the power of black music, responding both to its rhythm and the faith in experience it affirms."[20] The slaves used the spirituals to express righteous anger at their plight, to cry out to God for help, and to reclaim some of their traditions.[21] Slaves had been sepa-

[18] Ibid., 18.

[19] Ibid., 20.

[20] James Cone, *The Spirituals and the Blues: An Interpretation* (New York: Orbis Books, 1972), 4.

[21] Seay and Neely, 20.

rated from their homeland and their families, and often had witnessed their own flesh and blood beaten to death by their captors. They found in music a means to express grief, to cry out to a higher power, and to pass on stories of their horrific experiences so that future generations would never forget. Music was never a passive experience for the African slaves, and sometimes when the Spirit grabbed a hold of someone, that person became a frenzied dervish, dancing and singing and clapping. "It was in the wild release of a Holy Ghost visitation that the slave's Christianity fused with his musical heritage."[22] The Spirit was with the slaves, and their religious experiences testified to this loud and clear.

The blues and gospel music both sprouted from the spirituals in the late nineteenth-century post-Abolitionist era in America. Each of these musical forms, however, held its own distinct style and was nurtured in different soils. "Blues, descended directly from the gut-level emotional fervor of the spirituals, was melded with the work songs sung in the fields."[23] The promise and opportunity that comes with freedom was quickly extinguished for former slaves and their families in an unrelenting racist society. These struggles became grist for the musical mill that produced the blues. These songs were gritty, earthy, and blunt: "The blues themselves would quickly come to signify all the varieties of sin and suffering the flesh is heir to, from

[22] Ibid., 21.
[23] Ibid., 22.

whiskey to unrequited love, from existential angst to being down on your luck."[24] The flesh and spirit war continued with the blues. From a fervently religious people came songs that could tear the spirit in two. They were songs that told it like it was, including the variety of ways one could numb their pain through sex, alcohol, and drugs. Early blues artists like Howlin' Wolf, Robert Johnson, and Muddy Waters became heroes in the African American community, and later, in the white rock musician community too. There would be no rock and roll without the blues—no Eric Clapton, Jimmy Page, or Rolling Stones, or any of the hundreds of grunge, alternative, metal, and progressive bands they influenced. The blues are the meat and potatoes of the rock and roll stew, and its effect on popular music is immeasurable.[25]

Gospel music was in large part made widely popular by Thomas Dorsey, an itinerant preacher who began crafting religious songs on his piano in the early '20s.[26] Dorsey's background was in jazz and the blues, but he saw an op-

[24] Ibid., 23.

[25] The fact that many young music listeners now have no understanding of the roots of the music to which they listen is very troubling to some. Steve Van Zandt, guitarist in Bruce Springsteen's E Street Band, has developed a high school music curriculum that teaches history through music, explaining the cultural milestones that affected music (and vice versa), from the blues up to contemporary rock and roll. See David Brooks, "The Segmented Society," *New York Times* (November 20, 2007).

[26] Seay and Neely, 23.

portunity for marketing black religious music after the Depression decimated the blues and jazz music business. Soon, southern whites caught on to the gospel music craze as well and integrated this form into their evangelical Christian services. Gospel music certainly exerted an indelible effect on early rock and roll. Musicians such as Elvis Presley, Jerry Lee Lewis, and Carl Perkins were all brought up in the Southern evangelical tradition and they were very familiar with gospel hymns. Gospel music also exerted a substantial influence on the original music they wrote and performed. In fact, these three early rock and rollers, along with country music legend Johnny Cash, joined for an improvised session of gospel songs that was secretly taped by an engineer at Sun Studios in Memphis in 1956.[27] The gospel influence on rock and roll (and especially on its groovin' cousin R & B) migrated north as well. For example, Aretha Franklin's first "gig" was singing gospel music in her preacher father's church in Detroit.

These examples beg the question of whether there was a difference between the gospel music blacks and whites created in the early part of the twentieth century. Insofar as black gospel music was derived from the spirituals, which testified to the pain and suffering inflicted upon blacks during the time of slavery and even afterwards, then there was a significant difference, as whites did not endure a similar experience. How, then, did this difference manifest itself? According to rock historian Jim Curtis, "The

[27] Ibid., 50.

persecutions which blacks suffered gave their gospel singing a transcendent, other-worldly emphasis. To maintain
their belief in a better world after death, blacks made a
sharp distinction between sacred music and profane
music."[28] Certainly, some blacks preferred the dirt and
grime of the blues to the pristine, shiny sparkle of gospel.
If you are angry about being treated so horribly, sometimes
the last thing you want to do is praise God. The blues and
gospel undoubtedly influenced each other, but perhaps
fans of each did not want to admit how much. The flesh/
spirit dichotomy that haunted Christianity for hundreds
of years now inserted itself in the genesis of rock and roll.

"Spiritual schizophrenics" is a phrase that Seay and
Neely, authors of *Stairway to Heaven: The Spiritual Roots of
Rock 'N' Roll*, use to describe musicians within whom the
flesh and spirit battle raged most violently. Artists such as
Little Richard, Marvin Gaye, and Sam Cooke experienced
a strong religious upbringing, and their choice of career
set them in opposition to some of the values with which
they were raised—at least that is what they thought. The
inner struggle they experienced left a gaping hole in their
souls that they tried to fill, oftentimes with sex, alcohol,
and drugs. In their sober moments, the guilt about how
they anaesthetized their pain fed into a vicious cycle and

[28] Jim Curtis, *Rock Eras: Interpretations of Music and Society, 1954–1984*
(Bowling Green: Bowling Green State University Popular Press, 1987),
29.

increased their self-destructive behavior.[29] Several other artists throughout rock history have embraced faith radically, some even leaving their music careers completely to follow a calling.[30] At the heart of some of these conversion stories is a total rejection of what the artist believes is rock and roll's evil temptations. Jewish-born Bob Dylan converted to Christianity in the late '70s and his music started integrating Christian-influenced lyrics and even some gospel and soul musical styles. Many other artists have found a way to be more integrated human beings—to merge their love of rock and roll with a deep commitment to religious and spiritual practices without feeling that these are mutually exclusive. These are the artists, I believe, who discovered a way to find God in rock and roll music and in their creativity.[31]

What Would Jesus Listen To?

It is not surprising that, given its focus on rebellion and excess, some Christians feared rock and roll when it emerged as a popular genre in the 1950s. In the battle of the flesh versus the spirit, it was apparent to some which

[29] Seay and Neely, 96.

[30] One very highly publicized example of this is Cat Stevens, now called Yusef Islam, a popular folk rock artist from the 1970s who converted to Islam and gave up a career in popular music for over two decades. He recently began recording music again.

[31] I will return to this point in the chapter on spirituality and rock music.

side rock and roll took. Many Christian parents worried that the sight of Elvis shaking his hips, coupled with a rock and roll "primal" 4/4 beat, might encourage teenagers to engage in promiscuous behavior. Some of these parental worries were allayed with the birth of Christian rock. Christian rock music is, I believe, a fascinating phenomenon for a variety of reasons. I would like to examine the genesis of this music and some of its theological implications. My thesis is that Christian rock is a form of syncretism, that is, it involves the practice of embracing rituals that originate in pagan or foreign contexts and adopting them in a different form within Christian practice. One example of how this is done would be the way Christian rock music, given its appeal to young adults, is now used as an evangelization tool, provided it is "cleaned up" and presented in a Christian context. Christian rock provides one avenue for bringing religion and rock together, but there are, I believe, others that I will discuss in later chapters.

Christian rock grew out of "Contemporary Christian Music" or CCM, a genre popularized in the 1970s and 1980s by artists like Phil Keaggy, Amy Grant, Michael W. Smith, and John Elefante. The first Christian rockers had to fight against people who shared their faith but not their love for rock music. Many Christians did not see any redeeming value in rock and roll music, especially in the late 1960s and early 1970s when so many rock and rollers were embracing the drug scene. But this did not stop some from trying to baptize rock. Christian rock pioneer Larry Norman summed up the early attitudes of the nascent Christian rock movement with the title of his song "Why Should the Devil Have All the Good Music?"

Originally influenced by folk and gospel, CCM gradually incorporated elements of pop and rock music. The primary difference lies in the songs' lyrics, which are meant to evangelize, spread the good news of Jesus, and, presumably, win converts to the faith. This is chiefly why Christian rock draws so much criticism, because it sometimes appears to sacrifice musical quality in order to evangelize. Quoted in a 2002 article in the *Christian Century*, hard rock artist Frank Hart of the band Atomic Opera states that "he hates most Christian music because it is 'not art but propaganda.'"[32] And sometimes it is weak propaganda, incorporating simplistic "Jesus is my friend" piety and failing to posit any theological substance. But for all these criticisms and, perhaps, unfair characterizations that Christian rock endures, it is, according to a 2006 article on Beliefnet. com, the sixth most popular type of music in the United States, outselling both jazz and classical. What could have convinced evangelical Christians that rock and roll, once feared as the "Devil's music," could be something filled with grace? I would like to examine this question, along with some of the theology that informs Christian rock.

[32] Mark Allan Powell, "Jesus Climbs the Charts: The Business of Contemporary Christian Music," *Christian Century* (Dec. 18–31, 2002): 22.

Harper's Bible Dictionary defines syncretism as "either a conscious combining of two or more religions over a short period of time, or a process of absorption by one religion of elements of another over a long period of time. In both types the absorbed elements are usually transformed and given new meaning by the fresh context."[33] Christian rock seems to be an example of this phenomenon—by borrowing elements of rock music and absorbing them into a Christian context, thereby changing their meaning and intent. Rock and roll is not recognized as a formal organized religion, but it is exactly due to its similarities to a true religion that makes it so attractive to evangelical Christians. "To millions of devoted fans, rock doesn't simply deal with religion. Rock is religion. The freedom, the power, the rebel thrills, and the fierce hopes that rock music promises comprise a life-style that, for many, will always be more real than any truth revealed in a cathedral or ashram."[34] It is precisely because rock music holds a power to attract millions of devoted followers and inspire hope within them, like a major world religion can, that makes it so attractive as an evangelization tool for many Christians. It seems logical to assume that if Christianity could adopt elements of rock music, its power to enrapture its listeners would be transferred to Christianity as well.

---

[33] *Harper's Bible Dictionary*, "Syncretism" (San Francisco: Harper & Row, 1985), 1008.

[34] Seay and Neely, 7.

Early Christian music artists must have seen some transcendent qualities in rock music and likely themselves tapped into spiritual experiences catalyzed by rock music. Of course, all music potentially holds power to stir emotions and inspire spiritual experiences, but rock music has the added benefit of an enormous worldwide fan base, making it a very potent vehicle for spreading God's word. Christian rock, therefore, borrowed much from secular rock and roll music. Musically, contemporary Christian rock is indistinguishable from mainstream rock and roll. The same aggressive guitar riffs and driving drumbeats that religious listeners objected to fifty years ago can be found in contemporary songs by Christian bands like Jars of Clay, Third Day, and Audio Adrenaline. Christian rock such as this provides a more palatable "package" for a religious message. Instead of celebrating excess, a heavy and up-tempo Christian rock song will attempt to shift the listeners' attention and emotions toward a holier theme such as chastity or being born again.

Christian rock has also attempted to transform the culture around secular rock music. Secular rock music is often associated with sexual promiscuity, drug use, and rebelling against authority. Christian rock is attempting to direct listeners' passions away from these outlets and toward more "morally legitimate" practices. Christian rock bands will sometimes pray with their audiences, to remind them that in the end it is all about God. This can be difficult, obviously, in the midst of smoke and light shows that highlight the band above all else, but the intent seems to be to direct the emotional power of rock music toward praising God and away from self-indulgent behaviors. Through these practices we can see more than the hint of the flesh/ spirit split that Christianity has manifest in various forms throughout its history. It is to this now that I wish to turn, and examine some of the theological assumptions in Christian rock music.

Reformation Rock

The religious roots of Christian rock are largely Evangelical Protestant. While there are certainly many Catholics in the CCM fan base, I, as a Catholic music fan, have always felt uncomfortable listening to it. One reason for this discomfort lies in the foundational differences between Protestant and Catholic theology. Thomas Rausch, SJ, explains such differences cogently in his book *Being Catholic in a Culture of Choice*. Rausch writes that Protestant theology has traditionally been more "pessimistic" than Catholic theology regarding the holiness of the world. The "Catholic religious imagination," as portrayed by Fr. Andrew Greeley and others, helps Catholics to see the sacred in everyday life. The foundations of Protestant theology, however, focused on "Luther's personal struggle over justification or his righteousness before God," which according to Rausch, "has resulted in Protestant theology's stressing redemption more than incarnation."[35] This means that the world is

[35] Thomas P. Rausch, *Being Catholic in a Culture of Choice* (Collegeville, MN: Liturgical Press, 2006), 28.

more in need of being saved than it is good and holy. It makes sense that, if Christian rock emerged from this theological foundation, Evangelicals would consider it vital to "redeem" rock music by baptizing it with Christian lyrics for a Christian audience. Ironically, even with his theological struggles, Luther was an enormous fan of music!

Many strains of Evangelical Protestant theology also emphasize the "Word," or Scripture, as the source of revelation over tradition. "For Protestant theology, because of the corruption of human nature and its faculties, there is no 'natural' knowledge of God. God can be known only through Scripture, 'sola Scriptura,' through the intervention of the prophetic word."[36] As I wrote earlier, Christian rock is identical in many respects to secular or mainstream rock and roll music. Most, if not all, of the differences lie in the lyrics. The lyrics of a Christian rock song place the primacy of the Word tradition above all else and must communicate some biblically revealed truth in order to be legitimate. This, after all, is what separates Christian rock from secular rock, and the message of the music is also what Evangelicals believe make the music a powerful tool for proselytizing.

Mark Allan Powell highlights the themes that Christian rock has embraced over the past two decades. In the '80s, the genre took on a militaristic tone, perhaps inspired by the Cold War and the spurious dichotomy its supporters posited, namely, the Christian U.S. vs. the God-less or

---

[36] Ibid., 31.

Atheistic U.S.S.R. Christian rock in the '90s seemed to embrace topics that could have been lifted directly from a conservative evangelical politician's platform, but especially regarding abortion. "At least five songs were sung from the perspective of a fetus who, endowed with adult intelligence, knows that he or she are about to be aborted; in one case, the fetus asks Jesus to come into his heart so he or she becomes a Christian before being killed."[37] To be fair, secular rock songs can be just as vapid as some Christian rock. It doesn't matter if you are singing about your relationship with Jesus or your relationship with your girlfriend—if there is no talent base or creative inspiration, the result is going to be bad music.

While I believe my critique of Christian rock is justified, there are also some positive aspects to Christian rock music that I would like to mention. First, Christian rock served as a gateway to many forms of rock music for people in my generation. I know from speaking to dozens of people in my generation (Generation X) and younger that their introduction to rock music was through Christian rock because they were not allowed to listen to anything else. As teens, these women and men embraced Christian rock as their own, ironically utilizing it as a tool of rebellion against their parents. The band Stryper, for example, a Christian heavy metal band in the '80s, was popular with teenage boys especially, and helped inform their identity as music fans. Teenagers normally need to define themselves as autono-

[37] Powell, 24.

mous individuals, distinct beings from their parents, and there are plenty of avenues offered by popular culture to help in this regard. Christian rock provided an outlet for rebellion and self-definition for many teens, and gave them a taste of rock and roll music, thereby helping develop their musical palates for other styles of rock music.

Christian rock also attempted to ease the tension between religion and rock music. As discussed earlier in this chapter, at face value, rock and roll and Christianity do not seem to have much in common, and this has kept them at arm's length (or further) from each other for decades. Christian rock may have its flaws, but it has been a decent attempt at reconciling two "worlds" that were previously thought to be incompatible. As it develops as a style of rock music, it could perhaps open up new musical avenues for performers and listeners. Already, it seems that some mainstream rock musicians have discovered that it is acceptable and even desirable to sing about religious and spiritual themes without fearing criticism and accusations of "Bible-thumping." Even within the world of Christian rock, some bands are starting to reject this label, preferring to be known as "Christians who play in a rock band." Some of these contemporary bands, such as Switchfoot and Red, are interesting if only for their avoidance of the clichés often associated with Christian rock. If these and other rock artists feel that they can be people of faith and create credible music, they may have Christian rock to thank.

There are, I believe, other ways to bridge the gap between religion, spirituality, and rock music, specifically approaching it from a Catholic Christian spiritual perspective. Both rock music and Christianity have formed cultures with distinct vocabularies, lifestyles, and worldviews. As one who inhabits both of these cultures, I would like to try to explain how these two cultures can not only coexist but can also help each other without one co-opting the other. The either/or dichotomy that we have driven between Christianity and rock is unhelpful. It is a reflection of the flesh/spirit separation that Christianity has fought with for centuries. Both flesh and spirit are good, both are holy, and both can benefit the other. Rock and roll and Christianity mirror this relationship, and can do the same for each other. In chapter 2, I examine what some contemporary theologians have to say about music and how it can help one talk about God. I also explore some social and cultural commentators who have offered theological interpretations of rock music, some of which are rather sophisticated and may point the way to a new possibility for Christianity and rock music to relate in the twenty-first century.

Chapter 2

LISTENING TO GOD IN ROCK

I am walking through the central campus quad at the University of Michigan on my way to a meeting. I am lost in thought, trying to discern what I should say at this gathering, and, consequentially, not paying much attention to my surround-ings. My pace is steady but not rushed, and I feel the heavi-ness of my thoughts, causing me to direct my gaze downward on the chalk-scribbled concrete. I slowly emerge from the focused agenda on my mind and begin to notice my cadence—my feet dropping down at regular intervals and my rubber soles setting a soft, metronomic rhythm against the ground. A nearby construction site introduces the pounding of a jackhammer, which is sustained for a few seconds, then stops, then starts again continuously. Next I hear a bird calling from a nearby tree. I mentally put all of these sounds together and feel the resulting beat.

These are the rhythms of life that fill the background of most people's consciousness as they rush through a hectic day. But for a drummer, an identity I have proudly worn for half my life, these rhythms are something different. As one who relies on muscle "memory" and needs to genuinely feel something throughout his body in order to know it and play it, these moments when I sense the world's rhythms and meld them together help to hold me in the present like a Zen koan. I am drawn out of myself and experience some release of the burdens weighing on my mind.

In the last chapter, I argued that rock music and Christianity have fought a decades-long battle, echoing the centuries-old tension between the body or the "flesh" and the spirit. In this chapter, I want to illustrate why this tension need not be as pronounced as it is, and to suggest ways that rock music can communicate something about God. Rock can speak of God in a number of ways. First, it provides a negotiating space where the body and the spirit merge and can potentially inform each other. My story above is a small example of how I have experienced this integration as a rock drummer due to how my body interacts with rhythm and music. Much of this interaction relies on a sense of timing, a topic that theologian and musician Jeremy Begbie discusses at length. By utilizing Begbie's theology of time as it relates to music and the body, I hope to show how rock music can help a listener learn and talk about God in a different way.

Religious practice and spirituality can help people find meaning in their lives. Rock music also holds this power.

There are some similarities regarding how each of these draws a person toward meaning making, especially when confronted with the vagaries of life. One helpful framework for grasping this concept has been posited by theologian Clive Marsh. Marsh compares the meaning-making aspect of a theological tradition with the similar function of a music soundtrack. He reflects on how contemporary Christians are members of many different communities, including religious communities, and we seek a sense of meaning in several of these. Music is now a very common avenue for people to find community (for example, a fan base for a particular musician or group), and as a distinct mode of discovering meaning in life. Just as a movie soundtrack is meant to connect the viewer to the action and emotion conveyed on-screen, certain songs accompany people throughout their lives, connecting them to specific events, and these songs become their life "soundtrack." Some songs serve a cathartic function, others help people grieve, and still others mark celebrations. Given the importance of popular rock music to so many people, theology, Marsh posits, needs to find a way to speak to this mode of discovering meaning in the world and help people reflect on "the extent to which music (and especially popular music) accompanies and shapes living."[1]

Finally, I wish to examine what a few contemporary cultural critics are already saying about the intersection of theology and rock music. These commentators are not

[1] Clive Marsh, "Theology as 'Soundtrack': Popular Culture and Narratives of the Self," *Expository Times* 118.11 (2007): 537.

theologians, but they have discovered theological meaning within rock music and believe it important enough to express to others. Their work is interesting for a couple of reasons. First, it provides a glimpse into the popular language that people use to describe theological themes and experiences. Words such as "transcendence," "otherness," and "spiritual," while they may seem rather ambiguous and trite, are used by pop culture commentators to name something important about rock music. Rock connects some people with emotions and experiences that are not easy to explain. Theological reflection, I believe, could help grant listeners a new language for uncovering and expressing the "something" that happens in the interaction between rock music and the listener—and the rock musician for that matter.

While it may seem obvious, these accounts of rock and religion bridge building are also important because they provide a much-needed perspective on the religiosity of the listeners. Many hands have been wrung and many heads brought low by the often-reported collapse of organized religion in Western Europe and other economically advanced places in the world. Some in the United States fear that this increasing secularization will soon creep onto our shores and infect the young. The Catholic Church has proffered several responses to protect the institution from the secular "virus," such as promoting traditional popular devotions and bringing back the Latin Tridentine mass. These responses, I believe, rely on a narrow vision of what "religion" is and means in the contemporary Western world. Religion, spirituality, and a sense of tradition are obviously important for many in the community of rock music. The articles about rock and religion, the attempts at theological interpretations of contemporary music, and the increasing comfort expressed by musicians and listeners alike with cultivating spiritual language within the medium of rock music seem to indicate another part of the story that is often ignored. I will examine a few examples of rock music critiques that more than hint at theological imagining and describe why I believe these are important windows into how young adults especially seek religious and spiritual experiences through this medium.

The Rhythm Method: Keeping Theological Time

As I write this, I am listening to an album by the '90s rock band Live called *Secret Samadhi*. As my fingers cruise over the keys on my computer at various speeds, I realize that I am tapping my foot to the beat of the music. It is almost an involuntary response to the music's rhythms—sometimes gentle and smooth, sometimes furious and frantic. I used to drive my colleagues crazy during meetings in graduate school because I would tap out rock drumbeats with my pen on the table while others were talking. I meant no disrespect, and honestly I could repeat verbatim what anyone said. It was almost like a nervous tic that I could not control. How often have you experienced this? While listening to rock music on the radio in the car, have you started tapping your fingers on the steering wheel? At a rock concert, do you find that you can't help but clap along on the two and four beats during your favorite song's refrain? When this happens, you are expressing something about who you are and also possibly about how you experience God.

Perhaps you've heard the phrase "Live in the Now." It may have been co-opted and marketed by some self-help gurus, but this phrase reflects a basic theological tenet of many faiths, namely, the importance of being aware of the present moment. Jesuit priest Anthony DeMello, SJ, wrote that "spirituality means waking up." This means, among other things, paying attention to the world, emerging from under the avalanche of anxieties and pressures of life to savor being alive. We live so much of our lives in the past by regretting and in the future by worrying, that we lose what is going on here and now. Music can aid us in reclaiming the present moment, and I believe rock music is especially good for this because it is so visceral and listeners become more present to their bodies in space and time, in other words, more awake.

In our busy lives, we may think that time is our enemy —we're always racing "against" the clock and "fighting" time to get things done. Music, however, reminds us that time is an integral part of God's creation. Music is so dependent upon time and the arrangement of notes in a particular order in time, and it can help us as listeners to realize the beauty of time. Music, even frantic rock music, can help us to slow down and appreciate what is going on right now. This is embedded in the character of music, as

Jeremy Begbie points out: "The character of a piece of music is not given in an instant, or even a near-instant, but can be discovered only in and through time, and in some pieces only when it reaches a climactic gathering together, the end toward which it travels."[2] One cannot enjoy music of any kind without allowing it to unfold in time—whether the music is in the form of a three-minute-and-thirty-second rock song or a six-hour opera. There is no way to rush through a song because the arrangement of notes in a specific space of time is what makes the song what it is. To fully appreciate the song we must surrender to its claim on our time, for that is the very nature of music—it requires a sacrifice of our time. "Music," writes Begbie, "can be one of the most powerful and wonderful ways we have of enjoying, discovering, exploring, and interacting with the time and the time patterns God has imprinted in his physical world."[3] Once we surrender to music, it can reveal so much to us.

Begbie points out that music challenges the Western idea that faster is better. In the '80s when cassette tapes were the musical medium of choice, it was possible to fast-forward through a song while it was playing in order to get to a specific place in the song. Anyone who has done this knows that the song is incomprehensible and sounds a bit like Alvin and the Chipmunks. It is not possible to

[2] Jeremy Begbie, *Resounding Truth: Christian Wisdom in the World of Music* (Grand Rapids: Baker Academic, 2007), 220.

[3] Ibid., 221.

listen to a song unless we are willing to give ourselves to the time of the song. One of my pet peeves is when I hear a song I like on the radio and at some point realize that it has been edited to fit commercial radio, thus leaving out a bridge or an entire verse. Whether or not the artist agreed to his song being butchered to fit the commercial format of radio, the fact is that the song has been harmed in this process, and it has become less than what it was because of this tampering.

One simple but profound example of the importance of time that Begbie discusses is the Easter Triduum, where Christians celebrate the passion, death, and resurrection of Jesus Christ. These events, we are told from Scripture, occurred over a three-day period. Jesus was scourged, forced to carry the cross, crucified on Golgotha (a sweet name for a heavy metal band!), laid in a tomb, and rose from the dead on the third day. If these events happened as we read about them in the gospels, then it was spread out over three days. Through these days, Jesus' friends experienced a wide range of emotions, including fear, emotional pain, sadness, grief, anxiety, confusion, and finally, joy. Christians who celebrate the Triduum and give themselves to the mysteries of those three days can also experience this gamut of emotions. In fact, that is what this religious observance is all about. The Church in its wisdom follows these events in "real time"; in other words, we do not commemorate the passion, death, and resurrection of Jesus at a single one-hour worship service. "The only way that this extraordinary narrative will yield its meaning is quite simply if we play the events at their original speed—

God's speed, not ours—living in and through the events day by day."[4]

Music can help us appreciate how time works because it is so dependent upon time. Once we surrender ourselves to music, we must give ourselves to its time. This includes the tensions that are an integral part of music, as well as the joyful releases. We cannot skip over the uncomfortable tensions in a piece of music and only experience the release because it is impossible to have one without the other. From what would the listener be released if not the tension that preceded it? One of my favorite examples from the world of rock and roll of this interplay between tension and release occurs in the song "Won't Get Fooled Again" by The Who. The version at the end of The Who's documentary *The Kids Are Alright* is especially powerful. The song is a wild revelry. Everything about this song communicates a rebellious attitude, from the lyrics to the aggressive playing and the distorted guitar. About three-quarters of the way through the song, which up until this point has sustained a driving beat, the guitar, bass, and drums cease and are replaced by the droning sound of a synthesizer. The electronically programmed sounds lull the listeners, slowing down their pulse and providing a brief respite from the wild musical anarchy that precedes it. Suddenly, Keith Moon's wild drumming disrupts the respite. It sounds like he's hitting his lower tom drums with six arms in a machine-gun frenzy of notes. As the

[4] Jeremy Begbie, "Sound Theology," *Christian Century* (November 13, 2007): 20.

drums build, so does the tension in the listener. Just as the tension has built to a pinnacle, the listener is rewarded with one of the most gratifying releases in rock music—a boisterous explosion of sound punctuated by Roger Daltrey's barbaric howl that seems to come from another world. "Won't Get Fooled Again" is lengthy for a rock song, especially one that gets played on the radio regularly. But when a listener surrenders to the song and allows its time, tensions, and expressive elements to unfold naturally, the reward is extraordinary.

We are creatures who live in time—time that God created out of nothing, or *ex nihilo* (another sweet name for a metal band!). Music can help accentuate the beauty of the physical, created world by highlighting the wonder and importance of time. Listening to music, then, is a theological exercise because it reveals something of God to us. The ups and downs, joy and grief, consolation and desolation of life unfold in time. All of our experiences in time are powerful statements of how God is present to us. While God transcends time, we do not. But we need not view this as a limitation in our ability to know something of God. As a creation of God, time is blessed, and if we allow God's communication to us to unfold in time, even through an entire lifetime, it will affect how we embrace life. We will not be living in constant anticipation for something better (although some anticipation is also a necessary and blessed part of living in time), but instead we will be able to grow in appreciation for our place as creatures in time and of the wonder of time itself.

Reach out and Touch Me

If you have ever witnessed or been enveloped by a mosh pit at a rock concert, you know that it is rather chaotic, to say the least. Perhaps I am being overly sentimental in my analysis of the mosh pit, but I believe that we are often very uncomfortable within our own bodies and the longing for some physical human contact, which we often deny ourselves, can culminate for some in the frenzied environment of the mosh pit, where bodies are flailed at one another in an effort to feel the touch of another person. Tom Beaudoin and Brian Robinette address a similar theme in their 2009 article in *America*. Focusing on the physical nature of rock music, they write, "Listeners can also rediscover a rootedness in the body, while at the same time experiencing the body's expansion as it seems to fuse with the music."[5] This could be a possible way that rock music fans can negotiate a new way of being between the spirit and flesh. Feeling one's physical nature and enjoying the experience of pulsating beats and loud guitars transports the rock fan to a different realm—a more centered and even meditative state.

Chapter 1 discussed at length the battle between the flesh and the spirit that Christianity has hosted for two millennia. Rock music has been a victim of this battle and has faced harsh criticism because of its appeal to the flesh.

[5] Tom Beaudoin and Brian Robinette, "Stairway to Heaven: Can You be Saved by Rock 'n' Roll?" *America* 201, no. 11 (Oct. 26, 2009): 21.

But rock music could instead be the locus for an integration of the flesh and spirit. There is no doubt that rock music appeals to the emotions and the human spirit. It is also a very physical reality. Music can only be created by human beings using their bodies to strum, blow, pound, or finesse instruments, which themselves have been created by human hands. We are able to hear music because our bodies have this ability to interpret air molecules vibrating as distinct sounds. We hear a particular range of sound frequencies that make music physically possible. In other words, it is only through our physical nature that we are able to create and enjoy music. As Begbie points out, this realization should surface within us a strong sense of gratitude for the fact that music is possible. He writes that we should express gratitude "that there is a world where music can occur, that there is a reality we call 'matter' that oscillates and resonates, that there is sound, that there is rhythm built into the fabric of the world, that there is the miracle of the human body, which can receive and process sequences of tones."[6]

Listening to music should help us to appreciate that the world God created is, first and foremost, *good*. Music is not God—this belief would be idolatry—and not all music is equally good, but music can help us appreciate the beauty of God's creation and allow us a chance to savor the richness of that beauty and the miraculous nature of that creation. One of my favorite experiences that helps

[6] Begbie, *Resounding Truth*, 213.

me to appreciate the beauty of music as a result of God's
creation is when I discover a new rock band and immerse
myself in their work. It truly is akin to finding a personal-
ized gift that I slowly unwrap over the course of weeks or
months. I listen to a lot of music, so to find something new
and exciting after all this time truly blows me away. It
would seem that there are only so many arrangements of
a limited number of notes and scales—wouldn't we have
run out of combinations of these notes in all time signatures and rhythm combinations by now? This realization
illustrates to me that God's creation was not a one-time
act. Creation keeps happening, keeps unfolding throughout time, revealing many more facets to us. Through the
creation and enjoyment of music, we are drawn into the
sense of wonder about the nature of God and creation, and
the sense of goodness about the created world.

As a rock drummer, I find that these experiences are
even more pronounced. Begbie posits that "a plausible
account of music needs to take seriously its fundamental
embeddedness in the material world, its deep physicality,
as well as our embeddedness as physical creatures in the
world."[7] The physical nature of playing rock music, especially behind a drum kit, can put one face-to-face with both
abilities and limitations of the human body. These experiences can lead one to a greater appreciation for the physical
nature of rock music. I also find that I have developed a
keener sense of the subtleties of rock music by playing

[7] Ibid., 186.

drums. There are some songs where it seems an infinite number of things are happening in the space between the notes. These spaces help communicate the tension and release mechanism of music discussed earlier, and they are very important for a song's cohesion. Of utmost importance when playing drums in a rock band is to know when it is acceptable to play a flurry of notes in a fill or when to leave more space in the song. I can feel the anticipation that comes in-between notes and there is always a temptation to hurry through a part with a lot of "space." I consider it a spiritual discipline to lay back a bit and allow the music to dictate what comes next, not hurrying it and thereby doing damage to the song, but feeling the discomfort that sometimes accompanies this space, acknowledging it and trying to remember that it is a reminder of the physical nature of playing music—in all its beauty, complexity, and fallibility.

I find theologian Tom Beaudoin's description of playing rock and roll bass to be a perfect illustration of what I am attempting to communicate. "I discovered a sense of spirituality 'in the pocket,' playing tightly with a drummer. As a bass guitarist, when I am traversing the deep rhythm, riding the low notes, or stomping through a syncopated rumble, *something happens*." [8] The "something" that Beaudoin describes is not easy or perhaps even possible to define. What we can say about it, however, is that this

[8] Tom Beaudoin, *Virtual Faith: The Irreverent Spiritual Quest of Generation X* (San Francisco: Jossey-Bass, 1998), 14.

experience is only possible because of our physical body. We hear the music through the intricate mechanics of the inner ear, musicians play the notes on an instrument at the time they are supposed to be played with human hands, made possible by musculature, tendons, and ligaments, and we sing by forcing air through our chest to create vibrations that envelop our entire facial structure. All of this is only possible by utilizing our physical body and being open to the interplay of music with our body. Instead of fearing rock music because of its appeal to the senses and our physicality, we could hear and feel within rock a new mode of relating to and even understanding a bit about God and God's creation. Creation could have looked much different than it is—spending some time meditating on why creation is the way it is could be a valuable spiritual exercise. The creation of which we are a part is material and the modes of our interacting with this material reality can lead us to God. Rock music, I contend, is one of the more powerful and revealing modes.

The Soundtrack of Our Lives

Theology and organized religion in general have been accused of being out of touch with the contemporary world. Some of the blame for rapidly falling church attendance and disinterest among young adults regarding religious matters can certainly be placed on this lack of connection. Theologian Clive Marsh wisely posits that if Christian theology is going to say something meaningful to the modern world, it must meet people where they are at by addressing diverse communities' concerns in a meaningful way. One way that Marsh deftly approaches this vital agenda is by thinking and writing about popular media and how people interact with and are affected by it. In an excellent article published in 2007, Marsh discusses how theology is like a musical soundtrack in that it accompanies people through their lives, giving meaning to the trials, tribulations, and celebrations we all encounter. It is a great analogy, one that I believe is helpful to the discussion of how rock music and theology intersect.

To help understand how rock music can serve as a soundtrack throughout life, giving meaning to a person's experiences, I offer a brief example from my own life. I recently attended my twenty-year high school reunion. As a way to prepare for this occasion (and perhaps also out of a sense of nostalgia), I listened to some of the popular songs of 1988. Some of them I recall despising at the time, while others connected me immediately with some of the important events in my life that year. U2's album *The Joshua Tree* was huge, especially in the fall of '87 when I began my senior year, and those songs accompanied me through the entire year—dances, hanging out with friends, attending a retreat, and other meaningful experiences, some joyful and others painful. I still cannot listen to that album and not think of these twenty-year-old events. Since that time, rock music has become even more ubiquitous in Western culture. Marsh is correct to assume that, given rock music's presence in popular culture, along with its use by many people as a frame of meaning for their lives, it is vital to present it for theological analysis to help understand its power. The realization that rock music serves people by helping them articulate something about the meaning of their lives "invites consideration of the way that a theology functions for those who inhabit a religious tradition. It is the constant accompaniment of life—sometimes explicit, sometimes not."[9] Of course, not all people are believers, let alone Christians. This presents Christian theology with an even greater challenge—to be able to serve as a partner in dialogue with several sources of meaning to an increasingly secular world.[10]

Rather than fight against people finding meaning in a variety of places including rock music, Marsh posits that "the first thing Christian theology has to do in response is accept that this has happened."[11] The Christian theological community would do itself a favor by attending to things as they are rather than opining about how they should be. What is true in early twenty-first-century Western culture is that rock music provides a font of meaning for many throughout their lives. Rock music can connect listeners to a wider community, and it is emotionally moving to people, especially when associated with the important milestones of their lives. Rock music can no longer be written off as a

[9] Marsh, 537.

[10] For an excellent example of a self-identified agnostic who also utilizes the notion of rock music providing a soundtrack to score the meaningful events in life, see Neil Peart's *Travelling Music: The Soundtrack to My Life and Times* (ECW Press, 2004). Peart is the drummer for the Canadian rock band Rush.

[11] Marsh, 538.

"low culture" fad, or as a distraction. Christian theology needs to acknowledge that there are several sources of meaning for even those people who regularly attend church. Organized religion, while an important presence in people's lives, does not have a corner on this market. Rock concerts and fan clubs may not have replaced sacraments and liturgy, but there are more characteristics in common between these practices than some in the theological community would like to admit.[12]

In the novel *High Fidelity* by Nick Hornby, the lead character Rob wants to impress a girl he met while working as a DJ. To do this, he agonizes over making a "mix-tape" for her, which is a compilation of songs that mean a lot to him that he wishes to use to communicate how he feels about this girl without actually saying it. The process he describes is grueling, and a bit funny for those of us who have constructed a mix-tape: "A good compilation tape, like breaking up, is hard to do. You've got to kick off with a corker, to hold the attention, and then you've got to up it a notch, or cool it a notch . . . oh, there are loads of rules."[13] Imagine for a moment that Rob is an "on-again, off-again" church-

[12] There are several theologians, especially those born after Vatican II, who believe rock music to be a vital source of theological reflection. In my discussions with them, I have found that there is a lot of good thinking being done about the intersection of rock music and theology, but the academy has yet to fully embrace this as a serious form of theological scholarship.

[13] Nick Hornby, *High Fidelity* (New York: Berkley Publishing Group, 1995), 89.

goer. He skips church on Sundays if he has been out very late on Saturday night, but occasionally some guilt creeps into his conscience and he goes out of obligation so he can tell his parents he's "going to church" when they call. What if Rob was encouraged by his priest or minister to talk about the mix-tape he created with others in the church community? What if Rob was invited to describe why those particular songs are important to him, what sentiments he was trying to convey to the girl in whom he is interested, and how, generally, rock and roll provides a source of meaning in his life? And suppose that the priest/minister facilitating the discussion was able to provide Rob with some tools to do theological reflection on the varieties of meaning rock music holds for him. Unfortunately, as Marsh accurately points out, "churches often fail to encourage members to talk about what they are doing in most of their lives."[14] Theology, however, should do exactly that— give people tools to explore the meaning in their lives, which includes the way they spend their free time and the music to which they listen. Marsh is particularly astute regarding this point when he writes, "one of theology's responses to the ubiquity and influence of the arts, media and popular culture is to play its role in showing how churches have to be places (safe places) where theology and culture/theologies of culture can (must!) be explored."[15] This is a substantial challenge that Marsh lays before

[14] Marsh, 541.
[15] Ibid.

Christian theology. I wish to endorse it, encourage it, and, hopefully, aid it through this work.

Rock and Roll Theology

Marsh's challenge to contemporary Christian theology is an important one. Taking rock music seriously as a source of meaning is necessary if Christian theology is going to communicate something of relevance to the twenty-first-century world, and especially to young adults in the West. Rather than embarking upon a new avenue of scholarship, however, Christian theologians may find that they are instead playing "catch-up" with popular culture critics who have been commenting for years on the theological implications and meaning within rock music. In this section, I would like to examine a few examples of rock and roll musicians, journalists, and cultural commentators "doing theology." While these folks may not be utilizing the lingo of the academy, they are recognizing something special occurring in rock music that they are attempting to name and describe. Call it "spiritual" or "transcendent" or a special "energy"—whatever terminology they use, their point is that rock music can be a mode for talking about the divine. The first example I would like to utilize is the strong influence of Anglican liturgical music on one of the most popular forms of rock music in the 1970s.

Progressive rock music emerged in the late '60s and gained immense popularity through the '70s. This style of rock was born in England, although it quickly hopped across the Atlantic and thrilled music lovers in the United States. "Prog rock" is known for very complex arrangements, varying time signatures, and long, gloriously bombastic solos. While it is not true for every band, many prog rockers utilize keyboards, especially the organ, much more than other subgenres of rock and roll. Examples of early progressive rock bands include King Crimson, Jethro Tull, Emerson, Lake and Palmer, Yes, Genesis, and Pink Floyd. In his excellent and thoroughly researched book, *Rocking the Classics*, Edward Macan not only explains the emergence of progressive rock music but he also discusses the sociology of progressive rock and how its roots were heavily influenced by English culture. One of the institutions within that culture that Macan points to is the Anglican Church. Macan writes, "I believe if one wants to understand why the progressive rock style arose in England rather than the United States, one need look no farther than the obvious influence the Anglican choral tradition exerted on the genre."[16] Several of the prog rock pioneers, including Peter Gabriel (Genesis), Robert Fripp (King Crimson), John Wetton (King Crimson, Asia), and Chris Squire (Yes), regularly attended Anglican services as children, and a few of them even sang in the choir. This brand of liturgical music, which utilized a powerful mix of the pipe organ with the layered harmonies of human voices, stirred up strong emotions in the congregation.

[16] Edward Macan, *Rocking the Classics: English Progressive Rock and the Counterculture* (Oxford: Oxford University Press, 1997), 149.

Quoting Peter Gabriel, Macan emphasizes this point: "Peter Gabriel comments that . . . 'The organ in Chapel was magnificent and the playing was great . . . excellent. Everyone would stand up and scream their heads off . . . people would come out of Chapel feeling like they were on top of the world.'"[17] Macan draws a direct correlation between the foundational characteristics of prog rock music and liturgical music. Progressive rock musicians, according to Macan, attempt to harness this emotional power within Anglican liturgical music and interpret it for a rock and roll audience. "It is not unreasonable to suppose," writes Macan, "that some of the most notable aspects of the progressive rock sound—modal harmony, the emphasis on 'pipe organish' sonorities and quasi-choral vocal arrangements, the fondness for pure head tones and tempered singing—stem at least in part from the influence of Anglican Church music."[18]

Macan also posits that the progressive rock style of the '70s resembled a quasi-liturgy when performed live. He suggests two reasons for this: certainly the aforementioned influence of the Anglican choral style and use of the organ in this brand of liturgical music is a big one. Additionally, the visual effects that prog rock concerts integrated with their shows—lasers, fog machines, costumes—all added to the liturgical feel. Macan writes that these accoutrements "function in much the same way that candles and incense

[17] Ibid., 150.
[18] Ibid.

have in other religious rites throughout the centuries."[19]
The progressive rock live performance, like good Catholic
or Anglican liturgy, appeals to all of the senses and affirms
the goodness of creation. Another aspect Macan highlights
is progressive rock's tendency to emphasize the group in
a live performance rather than one superstar. Since he
borrows from Jim Curtis to emphasize this point, I'll go
directly to the source. "Religious music," according to
Curtis, "glorifies something greater than an individual, so
that the individual performers mostly serve as a medium
for the transmission of the music."[20] Given this reality,
people in the audience pay more attention to the music,
which is often very complex, rather than focusing on one
particular rock "demigod." Macan's analysis of prog rock
comes from his perspective as a professional musician and
teacher. While he is not trained in theology, his insights
about progressive rock's grounding in Anglican liturgical
traditions is quite sophisticated, and is just one example of
nontheologians reflecting theologically about rock music.

Another example of theological reflection on rock music
comes from Bill McGarvey, a singer/songwriter and the
former editor-in-chief of bustedhalo.com, a website for
"spiritual seekers in their 20s and 30s." In a 2007 article in
the British Catholic journal *The Tablet*, McGarvey argues

[19] Ibid., 67.

[20] Jim Curtis, *Rock Eras: Interpretations of Music and Society, 1954–1984*
(Bowling Green: Bowling Green State University Popular Press, 1987),
279.

that rock and roll music, specifically that of Bob Dylan, can express something important about our lives that we may find impossible to articulate. McGarvey expresses his distress about how in 1997 Cardinal Ratzinger (now Pope Benedict XVI) opposed plans for Bob Dylan to perform for John Paul II. Referring to Benedict, McGarvey writes, "For a Pope who has such a deep devotion to the works of such a classical giant as Mozart to have so little appreciation for one of the most important figures in twentieth and twenty-first century music is troubling and points to a lack of understanding of the scores of spiritual seekers—of which Dylan is a charter member—whose faith journeys might be somewhat messy."[21] McGarvey goes on to describe how Dylan's music provided him with his first truly religious experience when he was a high school student. It opened his mind and heart and when words failed, rock music provided him with a means to articulate his life joys and struggles.

I tried to make a similar point in an article I wrote for *America* magazine in 2000.[22] From my experience giving retreats to high school students for six months, I discovered how important music was to them, especially when it came to expressing their thoughts and feelings about God. When a student played a song that was very meaningful to her,

[21] Bill McGarvey, "Don't Think Twice, He's All Right," *The Tablet* (March 17, 2007), http://www.thetablet.co.uk/article/9497.

[22] David Nantais, "CDs Don't Kill People . . .," *America* 182, no. 1 (January 1, 2000): 14–15.

the other students were almost reverential, as if they knew something sacred was happening in their midst. It struck me that on three different retreats, at least one student used the Pink Floyd tune "Wish You Were Here" as a meditation song—one student even played it on his guitar. The song was not written specifically about God, but these students embraced it as a spiritual anthem to describe a longing for God that they felt. The take-home point I wish to make is that, when confronted with the question of what God means to a person, or how they express spirituality, popular music (including rock and roll) is a favorite means of articulating these transcendent themes.

Rock music should not replace other forms of religious expression or serve as a surrogate to a faith community. It should, however, be taken seriously as a mode of theological expression. McGarvey writes that he, like many other younger adults, did not make the mistake of thinking of rock musicians as prophets or gods. He writes, "I did, however, have a sense that through them I was able to catch some refracted ray of truth—something universal that can be hinted at only in great works of art."[23] This is an experience that the Church should celebrate, not dismiss. Just as a visual icon can facilitate an experience of God, especially among those of the Eastern Christian traditions, so too can rock music help people toward grace-filled moments in their lives. The Christian community could gain much by engaging in some theological reflection on

[23] McGarvey.

these experiences—reflection like McGarvey and others attempt in order to highlight the theological possibilities of rock music.

I have tried to explain how rock music can be mined for theological meaning. Rock music need not be an enemy of religion, or "baptized" to make it acceptable for the masses. It can be a conduit of theological meaning for us and allow us to more freely express that meaning in our lives. Theologians like Marsh and Begbie have made great strides in examining contemporary music and how it intersects with theology. But others, faith-filled people who are passionate about music, faith, and questions about God (in other words, all of us!), can also examine the rock music we love through a theological lens. Engaging in theological reflection within a group is one way to do this. Articulating our own theological and musical "soundtracks" of our own lives is another way. (I will be doing this in the final chapter.) All of us who have been emotionally moved, touched, healed, or challenged by rock music can find within it a theological meaning that could help us investigate the meaningfulness of our lives and our relationship with God.

In the Christian tradition, a popular way of cultivating a relationship with God is through its plethora of prayer styles and spiritualities. In chapter 3, I examine how rock music can itself be a "spiritual exercise" by drawing especially upon the spirituality of St. Ignatius Loyola. I will also report how some musicians have come face-to-face with their own sense of spirituality through playing, writing, and recording the music that we love. Again, while rock music and Christianity have not always enjoyed an amiable relationship, there is no reason why folks from both sides of the debate can't appreciate what the other has to offer.

Chapter 3

Spirituality and Rock Music: "A Fusion of Intimacies"[1]

In 1999 acclaimed director John Sayles released a film titled *Limbo*. The film stars David Straithairn as Joe Gastineau, a semidepressed Alaskan fisherman, and Mary Elizabeth Mastrantonio as an itinerant lounge singer and single mother named Donna De Angelo. In one scene early in the film, Joe asks Donna why she continues to struggle so hard to make a living as a singer. Her response is arresting and beautiful:

> Almost every night, it doesn't matter where I am or what song I'm singing, all of a sudden I'll hook into it. I'll be

[1] This is a phrase Patti Smith used to describe rock and roll in a March 12, 2007, Op-Ed piece in the *New York Times*. The article coincided with her induction into the Rock and Roll Hall of Fame.

feeling whatever the song is about and I can hear it, I can feel it in my voice, and I know that I am putting it across. . . . Moments of grace.

Donna's response reflects that she senses something special happening in the experience of connecting with an audience through the music she interprets for them every night. Her use of the phrase "Moments of grace" implies a transcendent experience, one that is simultaneously ethereal and mysterious, but also, by her description, seems very familiar too. While Donna does not explain exactly what she means by the phrase (perhaps her quietly passionate tone and the sublime look on her face was explanation enough), she describes in that scene an experience of connecting with something beyond herself. Music can be an avenue to grace, especially for those who have cultivated and sharpened their musical senses over years of listening, playing, and performing.

Jesuit priest Karl Rahner (sort of a rock star in his own right!) was quite familiar with experiences similar to those Donna described. He articulated a "theology of grace" in his *Foundations of Christian Faith* that serves as a useful hermeneutical lens through which to view these experiences. Grace is grounded in God's self-communication with humanity. Rahner explains that God desires to communicate God's self to human beings. God is not content to just create but desires a relationship with creation, one of "unsurpassable nearness."[2] He writes that God, "as the

[2] John Galvin, "The Invitation of Grace," in *A World of Grace*, ed. Leo J. O'Donovan (Washington DC: Georgetown University Press, 1995), 65.

abiding and holy mystery, as the incomprehensible ground of man's transcendent existence is not only the God of infinite distance, but also wants to be the God of absolute closeness in a true self-communication, and he is present in this way in the spiritual depths of our existence as well as the concreteness of our corporeal history."[3] A "Moment of grace," therefore, could be a spiritual event, one in which God draws ever closer to a human being through one or more of several spiritual pathways.

The experience Donna De Angelo describes could be one such event. Donna's description, "all of a sudden I'll hook into it," points toward an experience of something or someone other than herself. God's grace—God's self-communication—acting through the human medium of popular music is one possible explanation. For the musician, music is the means that allows for the experience of grace. It is as though the music cuts through any obstacles between the individual musician and the divine presence to reveal each authentically to the other. In this way, music is like an "aural icon" that can help facilitate a spiritual experience for the musician and help her to discover something that is both strange and familiar, both corporeal and spiritual, both felt and just out of reach. Performing or listening to music is one way the musician can experience God's gift of self. Just as a visual icon can facilitate an experience of God, especially among those of the Eastern

---

[3] Karl Rahner, *Foundations of Christian Faith* (New York: Crossroad, 1997), 137.

Christian traditions, so too can music do the same for musicians and listeners.

As a Jesuit, Karl Rahner was greatly influenced by St. Ignatius Loyola's *Spiritual Exercises*. Ignatius is very clear that God wants to be in an intimate relationship with us. We grab hold of things in our lives that can get in the way of that relationship. The Exercises are meant to help us let go of those things and make more room for God's grace. I believe that there are ways that rock music can be a spiritual exercise. I am utilizing Ignatius's definition of a spiritual exercise as "any means of preparing and disposing our soul to rid itself of all its disordered affections and then, after their removal, of seeking and finding God's will in the ordering of our life for the salvation of our soul."[4] It is important to note that while Ignatius outlines specific spiritual exercises in his manual, he always left generous latitude. He knew that his experience of God was unique. And while there are general spiritual movements within the Exercises that hundreds of thousands of human beings have experienced, they have not all arrived at the same place in the same way. It is possible, I believe, for rock music to help one enter into these spiritual movements. Especially for those who have been brought up listening to it, rock music can take people more deeply within themselves to reflect on their lives, relationships, the world, and God.

[4] George E. Ganss, SJ, *The Spiritual Exercises of Saint Ignatius* (St. Louis: Institute of Jesuit Sources, 1992), 21.

Once this happens, we are better able to see the ways our lives are ordered toward or away from God. We are then more able to choose what is most important to hang onto in life and what it is that we can let go of in order to be more liberated.

Rather than move through Ignatius's manual point by point, I would like to highlight a couple of his insights and reflect on how they could apply to rock music and its use as a spiritual exercise. Specifically, I will examine the notion of repetition and the importance Ignatius placed upon this in the Exercises. Utilizing contemporary psychology, as well as my own experience, I make the claim that the way one immerses into prayer is very similar to the way one listens to rock music. I also argue that, given rock music's connection to specific memories and emotions for many people, it can be utilized to help people be more connected with their affective life, their imagination, and, therefore, more connected to the movements Ignatius outlines in the *Spiritual Exercises*. Finally, I look at various expressions of spirituality in rock music and among rock musicians. These examples are meant to help encourage the reader to examine how rock music is important in your own spiritual life, and to experiment with ways of praying with it. I cannot be certain, but I think Ignatius would approve!

Before delving into Ignatian prayer, it would be good to review a few highlights of Ignatius's life that had a great impact on his spirituality. Ignatius was born in 1491 to a Basque noble family in Spain. According to his own auto-biography, he was quite a rabble-rouser in his younger years—a story not too dissimilar from some of the famous debaucherous tales of rock stars! His passion and desire for glory led him to become a soldier in the Spanish army. During a battle against the French, Ignatius suffered a horrible injury when a cannonball shattered his legs. He spent a number of weeks recuperating at his family's castle, and it was during this time that his thoughts turned toward God's glory and away from his own glory. Ignatius began asking what God might desire for him. He began paying attention to his inner life, noticing that some thoughts filled him with excitement, but then left him feeling empty. Others brought with them a gentle, sustained sense of calm. He realized that God was speaking to him through his affective life—his moods, emotions, feelings, and, of course, his intellect too. This began a long period of prayer, fasting, and penance for Ignatius as he tested the variety of movements or inner emotional experiences he encountered. He recorded his prayer experiences in a "manual," which later came to be known as the *Spiritual Exercises*. It is important to note that, while Ignatius was eventually ordained a Catholic priest and founded the Society of Jesus (Jesuits), he wrote this prayer manual as a layman who, at the time, was uncertain of his future course of life. He only knew that he desired to pursue God's will for him.

The *Spiritual Exercises* is a collection of prayer exercises, directives, and commonsense advice written for those who are guiding people on a retreat experience. Through his own trial and error in prayer, Ignatius learned a lot about the "movements" that human beings experience, such as feelings of consolation and desolation. These movements, if one pays attention to them, can help guide a person in his prayer, and even help him make good decisions in his life. In other words, they can help someone understand more deeply where God is acting in his life. I am greatly simplifying Ignatius's thought for the purposes of this book—scholars have been writing and discussing his work for hundreds of years and have found that, in many ways, Ignatius offered amazing insights into human nature and psychology (although he would never have described it that way). Two prayer methods in particular are important for the discussion of rock music and spirituality. The first is Ignatius's directive to perform "repetitions" during prayer. This means much more than just repeating something over and over. The second is the importance of using one's imagination in prayer. Ignatius's prayer exercises rely heavily on the human imagination and how the imagination taps into our emotions and desires. I believe that these methods of prayer can be enhanced by music, and that the way human beings listen to music is not only similar in many ways to how we pray but also can help us develop our prayer lives.

Play It Again

Have you ever had a few bars of a song playing over and over in your head and you could not get rid of it for hours or even days? Few things are as annoying as these "brainworms," a term that psychiatrist Oliver Sacks uses for them. These brainworms are most bothersome when the tune is a snippet from a commercial jingle or a syrupy pop song that you despise. While at times disturbing, this phenomenon appears to be quite common, according to Dr. Sacks. Sacks's most recent book, *Musicophilia*, offers helpful insights from case studies and psychological research about how music interacts with the brain. One insight in particular struck me as being related to Ignatian prayer:

> Our susceptibility to musical imagery indeed requires exceedingly sensitive and refined systems for perceiving and remembering music, systems far beyond anything in any nonhuman primate. These systems, it seems, are as sensitive to stimulation from internal sources—memories, emotions, associations—as to external music. *A tendency to spontaneous activity and repetition seems to be built into them in a way that has no analogue in other perceptual systems.*[5]

It would seem from Sacks's insights that we are "wired" for music. The human brain can grab hold of various perceptions and even recall them years after a particular experience is over. Musical memories occupy the human mind just as readily as emotional and experiential memories. We have the potential to recall music—snippets or even entire pieces—as well as the emotional associations

[5] Oliver Sacks, *Musicophilia: Tales of Music and the Brain* (New York: Alfred A. Knopf, 2007), 39; my emphasis.

with the music. To give a simple illustration, for those who are married, consider the associations with the song you and your spouse first danced to at your wedding reception. You can perhaps even "hear" the song in your mind, and as it resounds there, various emotions and memories rise to the surface of your consciousness.

In addition to these musical memories that are accessible to us, the brain seems to act on its own and repeats certain musical snippets over and over, even to the point of annoyance. Sacks illustrates that the mind is susceptible to glomming onto various musical phrases and will not let go, at least not on our command. Commercial jingles seem to be written by marketing companies solely for this purpose—to get stuck in a repetitive cycle in our minds until we either go crazy or purchase the advertised item. We are so wired for repetition that the brain can act on its own in this regard, without us actually willing it to do so. Is it possible that this drive to repetition can be something spiritually edifying instead of just getting us stuck in a mental rut?

Ignatius did not know about brainworms, but he did write about the importance of repetition. By repetition he did not mean simply repeating something over and over, but rather paying attention to one's inner reception of a prayer or memory or image, and staying put within the accompanying emotions until feeling satisfied. Ignatian repetition is an assimilation process whereby one pulls something external, such as a gospel passage, into one's personal and internal experience. Michael Ivens, SJ, explains the concept of Ignatian repetition with aplomb:

The Ignatian prayer of repetition is to be understood in relation to two inseparable processes: the gradual assimilation of the given material, and the development of prayer towards the simple, receptive and personal quality of contemplation. Repetition does not mean making an exercise over again. Though in the repetition one might replay some detail, or even pick up on a point previously overlooked or not reached, repetition is essentially concerned not with the material given, but with one's own significant responses to it, whether positive or negative. It is a selective and subjective prayer, spacious and unhurried, typified by the "pause," by staying put where "I find what I want [76]."[6]

This idea is rather radical, not only for its time, but also for ours. In many respects, Ignatius is addressing the question of what makes an effective prayer. Does rote memorization and recitation of a prayer draw us closer to God, or is it more fruitful to incorporate the prayer as a part of our spiritual lives in a personal way? His answer is certainly the latter. Ignatius wanted retreatants to not simply move through his spiritual exercises, but spend some time within them, playfully engaging them, wrestling with them, or being surprised by them—all of which are good, holy, and where God could be calling someone. This is why Ignatius left so much room for personal, subjective prayer experiences in the Exercises. No one can predict how God will be present

[6] Michael Ivens, *Understanding the Spiritual Exercises* (Trowbridge, Wiltshire: Cromwell Press, 1998), 58.

to any particular person. This is why the spiritual director's job is to stay out of the way! Or, using Ignatius's words, the director should be sure to allow the Creator to deal directly with the creature.

Ignatius counsels that one who is praying the Exercises needs to stay where he is until he is satisfied—this is at the heart of his notion of repetition. If I am addressing Jesus in my prayer and I find it consoling, or even challenging, it could be that God is inviting me to stay with that prayer until the graces of that prayer reveal themselves to me in their fullness—or at least as full as I am able to comprehend. Returning to the prayer is not, therefore, a simple repeating of the prayer, but going back to it and experiencing what it has to communicate in a different moment of time in your life. Perhaps you have had the experience of rehashing old stories with childhood friends. You recognize the stories, you have laughed at them before, but in the midst of someone telling it again you revel in it. It is still a funny story but it has not lost its luster just because you have heard it a number of times previously. Experiences of God, while often mysterious, can take on a familiarity—we begin to "know" what it is like to speak to God or Jesus as a friend. Returning to such a prayer serves to reinforce it and help one's prayer become more personal.

In the film *High Fidelity*, based on the novel by Nick Hornby, the main character, Rob Gordon, when asked by a friend if he has listened to a particular album, replies, "I haven't really absorbed that one yet." Music lovers can appreciate and identify with Rob's response. One cannot discern the merits of an album or a piece of music after listening to it once. You have to take time to listen repeatedly to the music, often replaying parts that are striking and consoling. By listening to music, one is trained to pay attention to the affective movements being stirred up inside. After listening repeatedly to a rock album, for example, it is much easier to actually "inhabit" the songs, to have them become part of one's life story and autobiographical musical soundtrack. This happens sometimes when a lyric resonates with your life experience, or when a melody begins playing gently in your mind, reminding you of a past event, even if you do not know why this connection is occurring. By paying attention to these moments, we train ourselves to become more self-aware and better able to notice what is happening inside of us, how God could be communicating with us. This is an incredible tool for prayer, for it aids our discovery of how God is touching our soul.

In the early 1990s a friend introduced me to Bob Dylan's music. I knew the popular songs that were in regular rotation on classic rock radio but not much else. My friend was a huge Dylan-phile and allowed me to borrow a number of his albums to get a taste of this musical icon's incredible body of work. Among many, one album that I really enjoyed was his 1989 release, *Oh Mercy*. I mentioned this to my friend when I returned his CDs and he concurred that it was one of his favorites too. About three months later, I was walking to the grocery store and a melodic phrase started playing in my mind. At first, I did not recognize the melody and I had no idea why it came to me. After almost a week of this rolling around in my head, it finally occurred to me that it was a line from the Dylan song "Where Teardrops Fall" off of *Oh Mercy*. As soon as I realized what song had been occupying my imagination for so long, I asked my friend if I could borrow *Oh Mercy* again. Upon listening to it again, I felt as though these songs were familiar, even comfortable, as though I had known them for years. I found incredible joy listening to this album, and my familiarity with the album seemed to have grown over the three months since I heard it last.

There is no way to know why a line from a Dylan song started playing in my mind three months after I had last heard it, and in many respects it does not matter. What does matter is that when it did occur, I was able to pay attention and allow the phrase to linger long enough to follow it to its source. Once there, I discovered great joy. I could have just as easily found some grief or pain, and that could have been good to face as well. For example, if the song I was internally humming was the favorite of a deceased loved one or a former companion with whom I had a nasty breakup, then that could have been God calling me to face a wound from the past because I was now ready. Ivens states that the process of repetition allows prayer to become more personal as the one praying assimilates God's word.[7] The dynamic of "getting into" a song

---

[7] Ibid., 96.

mirrors the prayer dynamic of the Exercises. As we actively listen to songs and pay attention to what is happening within us, the song gradually wanders through us, gently brushing up against a memory or perhaps loudly clashing with a long-forgotten emotional event. These occurrences are very important, and if we are attuned to them, they can aid our self-awareness and prayer.

Oliver Sacks testifies to music's power to stir up our emotions: "For many of us, the emotions induced by music may be overwhelming. A number of my friends who are intensely sensitive to music cannot have it on as background when they work; they must attend to music completely or turn it off, for it is too powerful to allow them to focus on other mental activities. States of ecstasy and rapture may lie in wait for us if we give ourselves totally to music."[8] Music does hold incredible power to tap into our emotional life and could therefore be a fine entrée into our spiritual life. One of the primary goals of the *Spiritual Exercises* is for a retreatant to pay closer attention to her inner life, especially the emotions. Ignatius is very clear in his "Introductory Explanations" for retreat directors that the one doing the Exercises should be experiencing "spiritual motions in his or her soul."[9] George Ganss, SJ, explains what Ignatius meant by the term "motions" or "mociones": "Motions is here Ignatius' technical term, taken from scholasticism, to designate the interior experiences, such as

[8] Sacks, 294.
[9] Ganss, 23.

thoughts, impulses, inclinations, urges, moods, consolations, desolations, and the like."[10] Ignatius was insistent that these "spiritual motions" were so integral to the Exercises that if a retreatant did not experience them, the director should wonder whether or not he is actually praying correctly. If recorded music had been around in the sixteenth century, it is very possible that, given its emotional power, Ignatius would have prescribed listening to music as a spiritual exercise.

Mining rock music for spiritual insights and practices is possible if we are, in the words of theologian Don Saliers, "attentive listeners" rather than "passive consumers."[11] Commercial jingles, music in elevators and grocery stores, and any other background noise are not likely to harness any spiritual power for us, especially if we are ignoring it. This is tempting to do in a music-saturated culture like ours—and sometimes it is necessary in order to keep our sanity! When we listen to rock music with attentive ears, however, it is possible to experience it as spiritual, as pointing to the divine. Saint Ignatius Loyola's notion of repetition in prayer is one means by which this can occur. Another is through the practice and use of our imaginations, also an Ignatian principle.

[10] Ibid., 144.

[11] Don E. Saliers, *Music and Theology* (Nashville: Abingdon Press, 2007), 67.

Is It Just My Imagination?

When I was a boy of about six or seven years of age, my mom introduced me to an experience that developed into a very spiritually edifying practice later in my life. She told me to lie down on the ground, close my eyes, and listen to classical music records. As I listened, I was to pay attention to the images that the music conjured in my mind. Once the piece was complete, my mom gave me some paper and crayons and told me to draw the images in my mind, whether they were actual objects or indescribable flurries of color. I enjoyed this activity especially for the freedom it afforded me. I was not graded on my work and I knew that whatever I produced on paper would be appreciated. Little did I know at the time that this exercise would help me develop my prayer life as a young adult.

Saint Ignatius's *Spiritual Exercises* prescribe meditations that rely heavily on the human imagination. Scripture is the foundation for Ignatian imaginative prayer. After reading a passage slowly and intentionally, one allows the imagination to picture the scene—what is the weather like, who is around, what does Jesus say? For example, Ignatius provides the following directive for praying with the Nativity story: "This is to see the persons; that is, to see Our Lady, Joseph, the maidservant, and the infant Jesus after his birth. I will make myself a poor little, and unworthy slave, gazing at them, contemplating them, and serving them in their needs, just as if I were there, with all possible respect and reverence."[12] This is obviously not the only way to pray, but it can be a very effective avenue toward getting in touch with emotions, desires, and the raw honesty that we must sometimes bring before God. This method of praying can be easy to do, or can prove to be difficult, depending on how much a person uses his imagination. My contention is that popular music can help one develop the imaginative capacity to enter into the meditations described in the Exercises.

Rock music can incite the imagination. By paying attention to our imagination when listening to rock music, we "work out" the imagination, training it and helping it develop. As we flex our imaginative muscles, we develop our capacity for integrating spiritual practices with our imagination as Ignatius describes in his Exercises. This is not to say that all of the scenes in our imagination are helpful or healthy—it is a matter of personal discernment which imaginations we choose to pursue and which we disregard. The more we use our imagination, however, the easier it can become to make a connection between the imagination and God's work through it.

What I am suggesting is not entirely novel. In their excellent prayer manual, *Meeting God in Virtual Reality*, Teresa Blythe and Daniel Wolpert apply the principles of imaginative prayer to television and film. "If you have ever watched a film or TV show and later imagined yourself somehow in the storyline, reacting and taking initiative to

---

[12] Ganss, 59.

change the outcome, then you know how to do this prayer!"[13] Blythe and Wolpert illustrate that one of the powers of visual media is that of flexing our imagination. The authors draw a connection between this practice and that of Ignatius of Loyola, who "urged those who underwent his retreat of spiritual exercises to allow the stories in Scripture to prod their imaginations, letting the biblical stories take on new life and direction in the heart of the retreatant."[14] Blythe and Wolpert then apply Ignatius's directives for imaginative prayer to particular films, inviting the reader to enter into the scene of the movie and speak to the characters. This practice could help someone enter into the scripturally based spiritual exercises—by starting with visual media that more overtly appeals to one's imagination, one may find it a more smooth transition toward applying the power of the imagination to Scripture.

How could rock music help develop the imagination to be more receptive to prayer and spiritual listening? Many readers may already know the answer to this question. What images conjure in your mind when you hear your favorite rock songs? Do the lyrics or mood of a song determine how it affects your imagination? It may seem sacrilegious or even silly, but when I prayed a meditation about hell that is in the *Spiritual Exercises*, I could not help

[13] Teresa Blythe and Daniel Wolpert, *Meeting God in Virtual Reality* (Nashville: Abingdon Press, 2004), 44.

[14] Ibid.

but recall images from a few of the heavy metal songs (and album covers) I have enjoyed for years! These images were influenced by music, but they drew from my own experiences and imagination of what the musicians were addressing in their songs. When MTV came on the scene in 1981, those of us who watched incessantly did, perhaps, damage some of our imaginative capacity. Instead of developing images in our creative imagination, we just absorbed the images that the artists or video directors claimed best encapsulated the meaning of the songs.

Legendary American composer Aaron Copland, in a book titled *Music and Imagination*, artfully sums up the power of music on our imaginative capacities: "Music as mathematics, music as architecture or as image, music in any static, seizable form has always held fascination for the lay mind. But as a musician, what fascinates me is the thought that by its very nature music invites imaginative treatment, and that the facts of music, so called, are only meaningful insofar as the imagination is given free play."[15] The visual arts, while requiring a great deal of creativity and imagination, can often communicate precise meaning much more overtly than music. Music demands imagination, according to Copland, "precisely because music provides the broadest possible vista for the imagination since it is the freest, the most abstract, the least fettered of all the arts."[16] Listening to music, even music with lyrics, invites

[15] Aaron Copland, *Music and Imagination* (Cambridge, MA: Harvard University Press, 1952), 7.

[16] Ibid.

imagination. The rhythm, meter, melody, and words can incite images, emotion, and desire. The imagination lights up, as in my childhood mind, with pictorial representations of whatever the music has evoked within me—some concrete objects, others wild flashes of color and bizarre geometries.

Jam On

In the rock music world, perhaps the quintessential style to appeal to the imagination is psychedelic rock music and its subsequent musical progeny.[17] Much psychedelic music includes long segments of instrumental jams, where guitarists noodle about on their fret boards and drummers go on autopilot, giving expression to whatever rhythm is aching to be released from their tense muscles. Psychedelic musicians and audience alike act as if they are in an ecstatic mystical state, dancing and twirling like dervishes with their eyes closed. It is not too surprising that the psychedelic music scene was associated with hallucinogenic drug use, although some fans refer to the music itself as "opening doors" in their mind and producing a euphoric effect. Drug use or no, the roots of psychedelic music and the culture that developed around this rock subgenre illustrate a strong influence on the human imagination and the

[17] The "jam bands" emerged from the psychedelic scene—originally led by the Grateful Dead; contemporary examples would be Phish, Gov't Mule, and Animal Collective. Other groups heavily influenced by psychedelic rock would be Mercury Rev and Kyuss.

power of rock music to tap into and even help develop the imagination.

No conversation of the psychedelic music scene can occur without mentioning San Francisco's Haight-Ashbury scene in the mid to late 1960s. Several foundational psychedelic rock bands rose from this rich culture, including the Grateful Dead, Jefferson Airplane, and Country Joe and the Fish. These bands created powerful and influential music, the effects of which are still felt in contemporary rock music. A novel artistic style was also born at this time, strongly influenced by psychedelic rock music and found primarily on the posters that advertised psychedelic rock concerts. In an article about the influence of Eastern religions on these posters, Kevin Moist describes an image of a typical psychedelic rock concert: "These concerts were fully interactive, involving elaborate experimental light shows that subsumed band and audience in a collective swirl of activity. The patrons were part of the experience as well, dressed in bizarre costumes seemingly drawn from some sort of archetypal historical consciousness."[18]

Moist's study is regarding how Eastern religions such as Buddhism and Taoism influenced the psychedelic rock scene, especially as evidenced in these dizzyingly colorful posters that local artists created to announce the concerts. It is not a far mental leap to make a connection between the

[18] Kevin M. Moist, "Dayglo Koans and Spiritual Renewal: 1960s Psychedelic Rock Concert Posters and the Broadening of American Spirituality," *Journal of Religion and Popular Culture* VII (Summer 2004).

unique artistic expression found on these posters and the imagination-stirring music that they announced. Mickey Hart, drummer for the Grateful Dead, posited such a connection: "The posters looked like what we were playing. They were an open call to come and have fun, which is what we were all about anyway." [19] Hart's words illustrate psychedelic music's power as a catalyst for the imagination.

One connection between these posters and the music they advertised is the stirring of imagination that psychedelic music causes. Psychedelic music's nonlinear and improvisational nature invites the mind to leap to a different way of inhabiting a musical experience. The ubiquitous verse-chorus-verse symmetry in a lot of rock music is disrupted in the psychedelic arena. Long instrumental passages do not have clean boundaries, so as listeners attempt to "get into" the experience, the music takes them on a journey within the imagination that they cannot anticipate. During such passages, if a listener is truly giving herself to the musical experience and at the same time trying to construct meaning for what she is hearing, the imagination is one of the only tools for this task. There are no lyrics to demand attention, only certain passages that stir emotion or try to musically express images and ideas. Just as my young mind conjured images, ideas, colors, and scenes while listening to classical music, some styles of rock music

---

[19] Mickey Hart, foreword to Stanley Mouse, *Freehand: The Art of Stanley Mouse* (Berkeley: SLG Books, 1993), 7. Quoted in Moist, "Dayglo Koans."

can readily accomplish the same goal and, in so doing, train one to practice his power of imagination. The effect of this practice on prayer can be great if one finds imaginative methods helpful.

Changing Tunes

There is a phenomenon in rock music that has fascinated me for quite some time. I have not seen much written about it even though it continues to occur. I am referring to rock musicians who "find religion," and often eschew their musical past. Some of these musicians have entered the world of Christian rock, others have changed the kind of music they make, and still others continue to create the type of music their fans have come to expect but begin being more overt about their religious practices. Here is a small sample of rock musicians who fall into these categories:

**Rock musicians who became "born again"
and left mainstream rock for Christian rock**

Artist	Mainstream band they left
Kerry Livgren	Kansas
Neal Morse	Spock's Beard
Brian Welch	Korn
Peter Baltes	Accept
Dave Hope	Kansas

Rock musicians who were "born again" or started being more overt about their faith in their music

Artist	Band
Nikko McBrain	Iron Maiden
Alice Cooper	Alice Cooper
Bob Dylan	(solo)
Al Green	(solo)
Van Morrison	(solo)
Prince	(solo)
Dave Mustaine	Megadeth
Gary Cherone	Extreme

When I read about rock musicians becoming "born again" and embracing a life of faith (usually Christianity in a majority of cases), I wonder how such a startling change comes about. There are likely personal, sociological, and psychological reasons involved, but my interest is in the spiritual reasons. Some may find that the rock lifestyle enjoyed by some (i.e., groupies, drugs, excessive alcohol use, grueling touring schedule) is not conducive to new priorities these musicians develop as they age. It is difficult to raise a family if one is wasted or on the road constantly. Other rockers eventually hit bottom and face their addictions—when they emerge clean and sober after a sabbatical, they may realize that the trappings of the rock business for one who struggles with addiction are too tempting to continue within its confines. These reasons may play a role—in fact, they do play a role in the lives of some of the musicians listed above. What, however, are the spiritual reasons for a change like this? It is a change that can sometimes remove one from the spotlight of fame and fortune in favor of a more modest lifestyle. Ultimately, the decision is personal—only the individual can explain the reasons for his or her actions. My desire is to posit a possible explanation based on rock music's power to put a musician in touch with the creative impulses within himself and somehow connect with a sense of the transcendent.

Neal Morse, formerly of Spock's Beard, is a good case study for this phenomenon. Spock's Beard is a neo-progressive band, heavily influenced by bands such as Kansas, Gentle Giant, Emerson, Lake and Palmer, and early Genesis. They gained a small but diehard group of fans throughout the '90s by writing great, melodic music with bizarre time signatures and long instrumental passages. They also gained a reputation as an amazing live band, which gave them a lot of "street cred" in the progressive rock world. Neal Morse left Spock's Beard soon after their highly acclaimed 2002 release, *Snow*. On his website nealmorse.com, there is an explanation for the impetus behind Morse's conversion and subsequent departure from the band:

> Morse came to realize that for him, embracing the Christian faith was the fulfillment of his spiritual quest. His walk was at once gradual and sudden—and as with so many,

completely unexpected. As he continued, his path increasingly revealed more of what his heart had sought all along. Yet he also began to find his career growing at odds with his faith. . . . Neal felt God calling him out of his former musical life and into the unknown. He made the agonizing decision to leave both Spock's Beard and Transatlantic. Despite having finally achieved the success he had long sought, Morse had to begin all over again: musically, emotionally and spiritually.[20]

After Morse amicably left Spock's Beard (the band continues today without him), he embarked on a solo career and has produced an incredible amount of material in a short time. His more recent music sounds very similar to his Spock's Beard material but lyrically it is more overtly Christian. Morse's first postconversion solo release, *Testimony*, is clearly his attempt to tell his conversion story to listeners. If this collection can be used as evidence, Morse clearly did not want to step outside of the progressive rock world. He even recruited close friend and Dream Theater drummer Mike Portnoy to play on the disc. Dream Theater have been the standard-bearers of heavy prog rock for almost two decades, so Portnoy's appearance on this album points to Morse's desire to continue exploring this rock subgenre, albeit with a Christian twist.

As I explained earlier in chapter 1, I as a Catholic have stayed at the margins of the Christian rock world, intrigued

---

[20] http://www.nealmorse.com/pages/biography.asp

by some of it and put off by other aspects. In an excellent essay on the subject of Catholic and Evangelical perspectives on Christian rock, Katie Oxx explains, "Catholics do not undergo the conversion experience so central to evangelical life, and some (many?) would resist the idea of a 'personal Jesus,' and focus instead on God and his creation."[21] Oxx explains further in a footnote in the same article, "It is through this experience (conversion) that Christians acknowledge their sinfulness and Christ's atonement for that sin."[22] This notion can certainly be found in Morse's first postconversion disc, where he explains how he emerged from a life of "debauchery," playing music all night and waking up hung over, to his acceptance of Jesus. All the while, these sentiments are paraded through a progressive rock backdrop. Given the centrality of this experience for Evangelical Christians and the animating force of one's conversion narrative, it makes some sense why musicians labeled with the "Christian rock" moniker would be so overt in their expression of religion and especially their personal relationship with Jesus Christ.

It also makes sense, in my own experience and from Oxx's insights, why Catholics would not be on the same page as Evangelicals on this issue. Intense and immediate conversion experiences are not typically part of the theological life of most Catholics. This is not to say that Catholic

---

[21] Katie Oxx, *The Mid-Atlantic Almanack* (March 2009): 80.
[22] Ibid., 85.

rock fans would eschew any hint of religion in their music. The contemporary rock band The Hold Steady have gained some attention in Catholic circles, not because they sing about the Real Presence in the Eucharist, but rather because their lead singer/guitarist and songwriter Craig Finn injects the band's songs with the Catholic imagination that I discussed in chapter 1. In an article in *America* magazine, the national Catholic weekly, Jesuit Sean Dempsey explains that Finn, as a graduate of Boston College, a Jesuit institution, was challenged by religious themes and ideas that influenced him enough to lyrically permeate his rock music to this day. "Although Finn does not currently consider himself a practicing Catholic, the grand themes of the faith stuck with him, especially the possibility of forgiveness and redemption in human life, despite the realities of personal and social sinfulness."[23] Subtlety in approach does not imply watered-down religion by any means. The themes of sinfulness and redemption could not be more central to the Christian life. It is a matter of how the message is musically packaged that makes a difference—and how that music itself contributes to communicating a theological point. Neal Morse and The Hold Steady should both continue to do what they do, for they do it well and thousands of people are being fed spiritually by their work.

[23] Sean Dempsey, SJ, "Hipster Orthodoxy: The rock 'n roll theology of Craig Finn and The Hold Steady," *America* 198:2 (January 21, 2008), online only.

It may help each to understand the other, however, and for their fans to do the same.

In chapter 4, I turn to the issue of social justice and how its themes permeate rock music. Especially for Catholics, but also growing in Evangelical circles, social justice is another central focal point for their practice of faith. It also serves, as I will argue, to build bridges with the secular world of rock and roll.

Chapter 4

LIVING IN HARMONY: SOCIAL JUSTICE AND ROCK MUSIC

In the summer of 1985, two rock concerts, held simultaneously in Philadelphia and London, raised over 280 million dollars for famine relief in Ethiopia. Live Aid, organized by former Boomtown Rats lead singer Bob Geldoff, featured some of the biggest names in rock music at the time from both sides of the pond. A reunited Led Zeppelin, U2, Tom Petty, Bob Dylan, and Queen delivered spectacular performances.[1] A number

---

[1] Watching YouTube clips of Queen's performance at Live Aid, I realized just how amazing their now deceased front man Freddy Mercury was as a musician and singer. Also a master showman, Mercury held tens of thousands of fans in the palm of his hand and lovingly delivered one of the best shows of his life. In 2005 a BBC poll declared Queen's performance at Live Aid to be the best live gig *ever*.

of the performances were broadcast on the then-nascent music network MTV, allowing people all over the world to watch some of their favorite rock stars jam for a good cause.

The year before Live Aid, Geldoff had assembled a group of UK rock royalty known as Band Aid to record a song called "Do They Know It's Christmas?"—also to raise money to fight poverty in Ethiopia. This effort was quickly followed up by "We Are the World," the Michael Jackson and Lionel Richie penned tune performed by the American super-group of pop stars known as "USA for Africa." Not to be outdone by their more mainstream brethren, a group of heavy metal artists led by Ronnie James Dio and dubbed "Hearing Aid" recorded a song for charity called "Stars." Through these efforts, rock stars, stereotypically cast as self-indulgent, narcissistic, and wild, showed that they could channel their passions for a greater cause and utilize rock music to do some good in the world.

One could be forgiven, however, for wondering if these efforts were undertaken solely to help those in need, or rather to raise the profiles of the rock stars that participated in them. The answer is probably somewhere in between and dependent upon the individual musician. What cannot be doubted, however, is that rock musicians have been involved in social justice movements for decades, well before the mid '80s, and music has often been used as a mode of self-expression against injustice. Some of this involvement is reflected in song lyrics. Look, for example, at the 1970 song "Ohio" by Crosby, Stills, Nash, and Young, written in response to the deaths of four Kent State University students, shot during a peaceful protest by U.S. National Guard members. This song became a rallying cry for the antiwar protest movement in the United States and highlighted the alienation that many young adults (and others) felt from their government.

There are a bevy of ways that rock stars have been involved in social justice causes, from animal rights and the environment to antiwar movements and critiques of the music industry itself. Some of these musicians, such as U2's singer Bono, use their high-profile image to raise awareness about important social justice issues around the globe. Bono has been able to use his popularity and influence to convince heads of state and corporation presidents to meet with him and discuss ways to help the less fortunate. These efforts go beyond simply performing a charity concert to raise money for fighting injustice. They show a true commitment to the common good and call upon rock music fans to get involved as well.

Perhaps it is not surprising that so many rock musicians become interested in social justice. Given the rebellious nature of the music, rock's ethos fits well with the movements that go against the grain, ruffle societal feathers, and, given its humble origins in slave hymns and American blues, focus on the common (wo)man. When Bruce Springsteen or John Mellencamp sing for the working-class man, no one is surprised and no one questions the legitimacy of their music. When Radiohead and the Beastie Boys speak out against the oppression of people in Tibet, it seems to many to be a logical extension of their roles as rock stars. But rock music itself has grown so large and commercial that it could perhaps be viewed as hypocritical for rock musicians to point fingers at the same monolithic corporations and groups that sponsor their tours and produce their CDs in environment-damaging plastic cases. Recent changes in the rock music industry regarding how music is created, marketed, and packaged have called attention to these specific justice issues. It also appears that there is a tension here between rock musicians and the industry that claims to support them, and one that will not be resolved facilely.

In this chapter, I explore the links, both strong and weak, between rock music and social justice. The first task is to present an explanation of what social justice is and highlight how mainstream Christianity has integrated social justice into its marrow. I will then examine the multiple ways rock music has inserted itself into the dialogue about social justice—from lyrical themes to social activism focused on the environment, critiques of big business, music piracy, poverty, and racism. Do any of these rock-inspired efforts have any effect on the listeners? Is it possible to enjoy music without being part of a consumerist culture? These are important questions for the contemporary rock fan, especially those who claim adherence to a religious creed.

Social Justice

For thousands of years philosophers of all traditions and backgrounds have examined the meaning of justice and have presented several viable and important perspectives. The Christian tradition has followed suit and has also posited ideas about what true justice is, not solely for the individual, but justice that looks toward the common good (social). Some trace Christianity's social justice tradition back to a specific chapter in the Gospel of Matthew, chapter 25. Here, Jesus addresses a group using parables, telling a story to make an important moral point. In verse 31 there is seemingly an abrupt shift in tone and Jesus begins talking about what the end of time will be like. When "the Son of Man" comes in all of his glory to judge who deserves to be included at his right hand, he will separate everyone ("the sheep from the goats"). Then Jesus explains the criteria for being judged as a faithful follower: "For I was hungry and you gave me food, I was thirsty and you gave me drink, a stranger and you welcomed me, naked and you clothed me, ill and you cared for me, in prison and you visited me."[2] Hearing this, the righteous will ask him, when did we see you hungry, thirsty, sick, or in prison and fulfill your needs? The answer is striking and alarmingly simple: "Amen, I say to you, whatever you did for one of these least brothers [and sisters] of mine, you did for me."[3]

Jesus' words are certainly not easy to digest. His message, however, is very clear and consistent through the gospels. Jesus is interested in how human beings use their material resources for the good of others to build a more

[2] New American Bible, Matt 25:35-36.
[3] Ibid., v. 40.

just world and work toward the coming of God's kingdom. Theologian Tom Beaudoin, in his book *Consuming Faith*, refers to Jesus as "God's economist" and presents two characteristics of what he calls Jesus' "economic spirituality." First, Jesus reminds us that everything of the world ultimately comes from God. We are not owners of the world's resources but, rather, stewards who are to responsibly use what has been given to us. Beaudoin writes, "Anyone who acts as though they have created all of their own 'wealth' has put themselves in place of God."[4] We must all keep aware that all good gifts come from God. When we start to believe that we are the ultimate creators of our good fortune, we are placing ourselves in a privileged position that belongs only to God.

The second lesson Jesus teaches is that the things of the world are for everyone, not to be hoarded only for our own use. Jesus' mandate is to think about those on the social and economic margins when we are considering how to use our resources. The early Christians, according to the Acts of the Apostles, implemented such a lifestyle when they shared all material goods in common so that no one went without the basic necessities of life. Beaudoin also highlights the writings of St. Paul and his admonition to the early Christian communities to not over-indulge at the early eucharistic meals.

[4] Tom Beaudoin, *Consuming Faith* (Lanham, MD: Sheed and Ward, 2003), 22.

The Catholic Church has taught that social justice is integral to Christian life and doctrine for over one hundred years. Starting in 1891 with Pope Leo XIII's social encyclical *Rerum Novarum*, Catholic social teaching has advanced some of the most important issues of the late nineteenth and early twentieth centuries. Workers' rights, economic justice, the role of the family, subsidiarity, and the common good have all been thoroughly addressed in this extensive body of faith-based social teaching. For the Catholic Church to express so passionately the responsibility of those with resources to give to those in need indicates the centrality of it to the faith. Other Christian denominations have followed suit, strengthening the connection between their faith and the promotion of justice throughout the world.

Secular rock and roll and the Roman Catholic Church might make strange bedfellows, but there is actually much agreement between them regarding social issues. The rest of this chapter will focus on these points of consent. As I have attempted to make clear in earlier chapters, my goal is not to "Christianize" secular rock music in some misplaced attempt to legitimize its existence. My goal is to highlight the ways rock and roll music, in all its secular glory, can reveal hints of the divine to its fans. This occurs in several ways, and congruence on social justice issues between Christian teaching and the more secular-humanist perspective found in rock music is an important one. Along the way, we may even find that the more "secular" milieu of rock music can teach religion something about social justice.

(Eco-) System of a Down

Serj Tankian is front man for the hard rock band System of a Down as well as one of the most passionate contemporary rock musician social justice activists. Serj, along with Rage Against the Machine guitarist Tom Morello, founded a nonprofit organization called Axis of Justice (axisofjustice.net) "to bring together musicians, fans of music, and grassroots political organizations to fight for social justice."[5] The organization website encourages rock fans to get involved in any number of social justice issues, many of which are not widely publicized in the mainstream media. Axis is currently working to have the Armenian genocide recognized as such around the world, as well as leading the fight for fair wages for workers at Korean guitar manufacturing plants. This latter cause is an interesting one because it also encourages rock musicians, from the amateur to the seasoned pro, to think about what instruments they use, where they are made, and who is benefiting from their sale. Their website also contains a number of important resources for longtime and would-be activists who want to join in the struggle for the common good. It also provides links to social justice-themed songs from the past forty years.

One of Tankian's primary passions these days is preserving the environment, but not through the usual avenues green advocates take. Tankian is concerned about

[5] http://axisofjustice.net/about/

how the hundreds of bombs dropped on the Middle East in the Iraq and Afghanistan wars affect the topsoil in those areas. The ecosystem in the Middle East, he laments in an article in the *New York Times*, could be permanently damaged. Tankian's efforts to help the environment have been both creative and groundbreaking. Rather than just reduce waste and sell ecofriendly items at his concert "merch" table, Tankian sees a connection between war, poverty, and the environment; he does not believe it is possible to address only one of these issues. He states, "Even materials that are supposed to be environmentally friendly can be harmful to poor communities. Biodiesel, for example, uses up farmland that could otherwise be used to grow food for starving people."[6]

Tankian possesses the unique ability to avoid the holier-than-thou attitude that can infect some social activists. Likely, this comes from his own self-awareness that he can be part of the problem as much as the solution. Any touring rock musician leaves a large carbon footprint, whether traveling by bus or plane. Tankian attempts to offset this by using locally grown organic food backstage at his shows, providing recycling bins at all shows, and allowing fans to purchase energy credits to offset their travel to the concert venue. One fascinating idea Tankian posits is "holographic touring" as a way to reduce the negative

[6] Cortney Harding, "Q&A: Rocker Tankian spreads the word on social justice," Reuters (March 22, 2008), http://www.reuters.com/article/idUSN2222676220080324.

environmental impact of rock shows. "For instance," he states, "I have a studio next to my house and a live performance room in the studio. I could broadcast a show in real time and could interact with the audience as if we were in the same room."[7] This type of creative thinking by a rock star could revolutionize the music industry and make it more "green" in the process.[8] And even if it is not possible, it still demonstrates that he is thinking outside the box about these important issues and how they are interconnected.

When I was a graduate student studying biochemistry at Iowa State University in Ames, Iowa, I worked as a lab assistant for about fifty hours per week. To balance this very cerebral work (and to earn some extra cash), I found a second job as a "local roadie" helping set up for rock shows that would regularly come through Ames. One show I worked was the Pretenders, the '70s post-punk band led by snarling female vocalist and songwriter Chrissy Hynde. It is well known in the rock world that Hynde is a very passionate animal rights activist who practices vegetarianism. What I found interesting was that the catering company that fed the band and crew (myself included) served only low-fat vegetarian fare per Hynde's request. If she was paying for it, she was going to control what even the local hired help was eating. At the time, I was a vegetarian

[7] Ibid.

[8] Speaking of "green" performances, a black metal band called Wolves in the Throne Room performs their concerts in the forests of the West Coast. Erik Davis, "Deep Eco-Metal," *Slate* (November 13, 2007).

myself and I did not mind—and as a poor graduate student I was just grateful for the free grub! Now in retrospect I wonder how many people would see this as a heavy-handed attempt to promote an issue, or even an abuse of power. This is just to say that if high-profile rock stars promote social justice issues, this does not take away fans' responsibility to look critically at issues themselves. I do not want to suggest that Hynde was wrong to dictate the food served backstage at her gigs, but only to say that fans should keep a critical eye on what rock stars are saying and doing. Allowing popularity to dictate truth can be dangerous.

Rock stars have also addressed ecological themes through the lyrics of their music. Sometimes songwriters do this to raise concerns about environmental destruction and other times nature is used as a metaphor for a spiritual connection with something greater than themselves. "Mercy, Mercy Me (The Ecology)" by Marvin Gaye is one of the most famous songs that addresses environmental concerns. The Beatles, according to one scholar, used the symbols sun and home in a number of their tunes. "The use of 'home' and 'sun' as metaphors of an archetypal return resonates with writers and poets from all ages and cultures. The journey and return home from a place of exile or alienation is often aligned with conscious or unconscious transformations."[9] These quasi-mystical lyrics signal a

[9] Dirk Dunbar, "The Evolution of Rock and Roll: Its Religious and Ecological Themes," *Journal of Religion and Popular Culture* II (Fall 2002): 13.

desire to find a source of stability in nature during a time of social upheaval. The Moody Blues, also a musical force in the late '60s and early '70s, focused on the sacredness of the environment in a number of their songs. "The notion of a journey through life, the cosmos, and back home permeates each album; and home, the sun, and a sacred earth serve as dominant themes and/or metaphors."[10]

I suggest that these themes point to a desire to connect with nature in a spiritual way, to strip away the complexities of the modern industrial society and find a "home" in what is perceived as a simpler, more pure milieu. There is a strong history within the Christian tradition (and others) to find spiritual nourishment in nature. Teilhard de Chardin, a Jesuit paleontologist who wrote extensively about religion and science, was able to make startling connections between evolution in nature and God's ongoing creative work in the universe. His descriptions of finding God's holy work in the natural world are prime examples of how compatible the Christian tradition can be with working for environmental justice.

Rock stars who are environmental activists may be surprised to find a lot of common ground with mainstream Christianity. While there has never been a papal encyclical on the environment, social ethicist Thomas Massaro, SJ, sees trends in Catholic social thought that point to mounting support for caring for the earth and its dwindling resources. He writes, "Many parishes and dioceses have adopted programs to raise awareness of pollution and to organize efforts to preserve our fragile ecosystem. Local campaigns to expand recycling, encourage organic farming, and raise funds to preserve the world's shrinking rain forests have often been started or sponsored by churches."[11] Jim Wallis, popular author and speaker, and founder of *Sojourners* magazine, recently noted that Evangelical Christians, who have often been characterized as caring only about prayer in schools and abortion, are passionately embracing environmentalism as a twenty-first-century concern. In his blog in the *Washington Post*, Wallis writes, "The concern over global warming, in particular, is even stronger among a new generation of young evangelicals who have made environmental stewardship a mainstream and virtually consensus issue among their peers. Evangelicals tell me that global warming is a 'life issue' for them and a fundamental part of Christian ethics."[12] Young adult Christians, many of whom are rock fans, are shifting the social justice landscape in their faith communities and addressing issues that are pertinent to their generations.

This is not to suggest that rock fans always embrace the social justice issues that their favorite musicians advocate, but these issues would not have such a high profile

[11] Thomas Massaro, SJ, *Living Justice: Catholic Social Teaching in Action* (Lanham, MD: Rowman and Littlefield, 2000), 227.

[12] Jim Wallis, "Evangelicals: A Tipping Point on the Environment?" *Washington Post* Blog "On Faith," http://newsweek.washingtonpost.com/onfaith/panelists/jim_wallis/2007/02/evangelicals_a_tipping_point_o.html.

among the rock fan base if not for famous rock stars promoting them. If a rock fan embraces environmental concerns because his faith impels him or because his favorite band promotes it, does it really matter? It could be a point of synergy between one's faith and real life concerns, and that only promotes a healthy spirituality. There are other social justice issues that may or may not be obvious to rock and roll fans because they have to do with the popular music industry itself. In this next section, I will address two of these: commercialism and music ownership.

Rock for Sale

"The great insanity of our times," posited Win Butler, leader of the Canadian rock band Arcade Fire, ". . . is this idea that Christianity and consumerism are completely compatible."[13] Butler may have a valid point regarding Christianity, but it seems that consumerism and the rock music industry have a tight-knit relationship and will not be breaking up anytime soon. Some popular rock musicians, such as Arcade Fire, Aimee Mann, and Prince, have attempted to avoid the "big business" of the rock music industry by releasing their music on independent labels and selling albums through their websites. This practice may steer clear of one aspect of the rock music industry and avoid the "middleman," but it certainly does not step

[13] Greg Kot, "Band of the Year: An Interview with Arcade Fire," http://www.popmatters.com/pm/feature/band-of-the-year-an-interview-with-the-arcade-fire.

outside of consumer culture. Fans must still purchase music from these artists within a capitalist system that is open to economic, sociological, and theological critique. When rock musicians are able to connect directly with the fans without passing their music through the commercial industry filter, they can establish a more intimate relationship with them and often they can release music that is more true to their creative impulses rather than meeting some executive order to produce a popular single. They must still, however, market the music and attempt to appeal to fans within our economic system. I cannot hope to unravel the multitude of issues that emerge from the relationship of consumer capitalism and the rock music world; however, I will wade briefly into these murky waters in the hopes of catalyzing discussions about these issues among rock music fans.

Another theologian who has deftly commented on the consumer culture in the Western world is Vincent Miller. His book *Consuming Religion* is invaluable for understanding how our consumerist habits affect our religious practice. Commenting on our society's search for meaning and identity, Miller writes, "As clan, family, profession, and other sources of ascribed identity have faded in significance, consumption has become the major means by which people establish, maintain, and communicate their personal and social identities."[14] The rock music industry takes advantage of this reality as much as any other. To be

[14] Vincent J. Miller, *Consuming Religion* (New York: Continuum, 2003), 49.

a member of the community of fans of any rock band requires (many believe) purchasing T-shirts, posters, ring tones, shot glasses, and whatever other merchandise the band chooses to paste its name on. This is not even to mention the multiple versions of albums—extended mixes, remixes, "lost" tracks, and B-sides. As one example, my friend Dan commented on how he has felt manipulated by the rock music industry with regard to purchasing multiple copies of the same album. He noted wryly that he has purchased about six versions of "Live at Leeds" by The Who, which is regarded as one of the greatest recorded live rock performances of all time. He bought it first on vinyl in the '80s, then on CD, then he was persuaded to pick up the remastered version a few years later, followed soon after by the "special" two-disc set that included un-released live tracks from the same show. After listing the various incarnations of the same songs that he had pur-chased, he announced, with much frustration in his voice, "I'm not buying that album again!"

Often it is the record company's, not the artist's, deci-sion to release multiple copies of the same collection of songs. This is not to absolve all rock artists from taking advantage of the rabid nature of some of their fans. Unlike my friend Dan, many fans *will* purchase every possible collection of music. Bands and record companies alike understand this and take advantage of it for financial gain. The Doors, a popular rock band in the late '60s led by the now-deceased charismatic and troubled lead singer Jim Morrison, continues to sell thousands of copies of the multiple "Greatest Hits" and "Best of" collections that its record company has released over the decades. I love The Doors and I could never disparage their musicianship, but how many versions of "Light My Fire" or "Riders on the Storm" does one person really need? The fact that thousands of fans *do* purchase these same songs over and over again points to the truth contained in Miller's words. We are dependent upon consumerism to create our social identities. In this case the identity is that of "rock music fan" and the social currency that comes along with it—identity as a "rebel" or a sort of guru-like status that often accompanies the most fanatic followers of rock bands.

Miller explains that our drive to consume goods, be they from the rock music industry or others, "is driven as much by social necessity and anxiety as by desire."[15] The longing for a social identity and a desire to "fit in" with a group is what the rock music industry takes advantage of to sell goods. This has especially been true since the advent of music videos, which served to make image more important than the music. Now the music industry sells sex appeal, glamour, and "gangster" images rather than focusing on musical quality. Even Christian rock, ironically, appeals to this sense of anxiety to fit in with a social group. Christian rock is closely related enough to secular rock music to provide an easily identified social category to fill the need in the teen or young adult's life for "belonging" to a group. For example, Christian heavy metal bands in the late '80s

[15] Ibid., 116.

looked a lot like their mainstream counterparts—the spandex, the long hair, the disheveled appearance, and even eye makeup! The image was close enough to be readily identified by their target audience, but different enough for the music to become its own subgenre under the category of rock music, and thus for the fans to form their own social identity. It is ironic because these same young fans would have found social identity through their institutional churches decades ago, but now find it through the medium of popular culture.

Given the importance of identity with a community, those of us who self-identify as Christian need to be thoughtful regarding from where we draw that identity. Christian identity impels believers to look upon the poor and oppressed as brothers and sisters, not as outcasts. The choices we as Christians make regarding how we spend our money and what we spend it on are spiritual choices requiring prayerful discernment. Impulsive spending encourages an identity that is other than Christian and can be harmful not only to our spiritual lives but also to those in need who will continue to be forgotten. Tom Massaro, SJ, also poses an important challenge to the conspicuous consumption sometimes present in the rock music industry. "Is each person," he writes, "to be understood as a consuming individual, as merely a bundle of selfish and infinite desires?"[16] Catholic social teaching, Massaro illustrates, answers no! I contend that it offers a view of the human

[16] *Living Justice*, 192.

person that could help those of us who have no intention of giving up rock music to reimagine what rock fandom could be. The rock music industry can, at times, manipulate us into thinking that we "need" that T-shirt or that remastered compact disc in order to be happy. Not only is it prudent to exercise some spiritual discernment in what music merchandise we purchase but we should also be concerned with bigger questions regarding how our spending affects others. We are relational beings and we do have moral obligations toward people we do not know, especially those who are on the economic margins of our world.[17]

Listening Local

I am not a proponent of demonizing record companies, but there is no doubt the industry has changed. In an article about record producer Rick Rubin in the *New York Times Magazine*, Lynn Hirschberg quotes from industry king David Geffen about the evolution of the industry. "Only 10 years ago, companies wanted to make records, presumably good records, and see if they sold. But panic has set in, and now it's no longer about making music, it's all about how to sell music."[18] For one of the industry's leading

[17] See Beaudoin's *Consuming Faith* for a more in-depth discussion of this point.

[18] Lynn Hirschberg, "The Music Man," *New York Times Magazine* (September 2, 2007): 28.

businessmen to say this is a big deal. The music that the industry produces and releases to the public must be affected by this laser-like focus on the bottom line. What can rock fans do about this, short of stopping listening to music altogether? Is it possible that rock fans concerned with economic justice can exercise some influence with their musical passions and make a difference?

I am proposing that rock fans could learn a lesson from the "buy local" movement so prominent now in the food industry. The benefits to purchasing organic meat and produce from local farmers are multiple. Two in particular are that it stimulates the local economy and allows a local farmer to be able to compete with big agri-business, and it protects the environment by cutting down on the use of trucks to transport food across the country. From my personal experience of purchasing food from local farmers within one hundred miles of the city of Detroit, it is clear that promoting locally grown food also educates locals about where their food comes from and about proper nutrition. These benefits seem very positive, but what does the "buy local" movement have to do with rock music?

As a rock drummer who has played in multiple bands in various cities for over two decades, I can attest to the incredible musical creativity bubbling up around the United States. This should not be news to most rock fans— just open a local pop culture newspaper in your city and check out the listings of local bands playing at venues less than fifteen miles away. These bands are comprised of local "weekend warriors" of all ages who carve out time in their schedules among work and familial obligations in an effort to create something new and exciting. No, we don't always succeed, but the effort and desire are genuine.

For those rock fans who want to find some new, quality music, I suggest choosing a local band and paying the five-, eight-, or ten-dollar cover to support them. Doing this over a period of months will not only support the local economy and encourage local musicians to continue making music but it is also very likely that you will truly enjoy a few of these bands and become a fan. Even the shows you do not enjoy will still result in supporting the economy and offers an opportunity to hang with the local community of fans. In her book about music and ethics, Kathleen Higgins explains that one of the most obvious intersections between music and ethics is in regard to the context in which the music is heard, specifically, in the presence of other people. She writes, "One of the most important and most obvious cross-cultural values of music is its power to induce social cohesion. Music brings people together, and the way in which it brings people together often impresses them as profound."[19] I would argue that this social cohesion is even more possible on the local rock scene, where venues are much smaller and the audience often lives nearby.

The music industry releases only so many singles and albums each year and a majority of the public only hears a sliver that someone in the industry believes will make

[19] Kathleen Higgins, *The Music of our Lives* (Philadelphia: Temple University Press, 1991), 18.

money regardless of quality. Many local musicians are craving to have their material heard and some are even open to feedback from listeners. In this way, the process of creating music becomes much more "organic" and open to evolving rather than being produced in response to perceived popular tastes. Listening local also sends a message to the big recording companies that much of the material they release is not what a large segment of the population desires to hear.

Electric Purgatory

In chapter 1, I wrote about the African American roots of rock and roll. Any discussion of social justice and rock music must include a discussion of race and racism. In the rock and roll world, race is the elephant in the recording studio. If one were to randomly ask people walking down the street in Anytown, U.S.A., what they consider "white" music and what they consider "black" music, rock and roll would inevitably fall under the former. Rap, R & B, and even jazz would be labeled as "black" music. But rock's origins are in the African American culture. Gospel and blues, the styles from which rock and roll was born, are musical inventions of the black community. Ask those same residents of Anytown if they can list examples of African American rock musicians and you would hear very few— Chuck Berry, Jimi Hendrix, Living Colour, and maybe (from the savvy rock fans) Fishbone. How is this possible given the enormous influence of African Americans on the creation of rock and roll?

In 1985, Vernon Reid, guitarist for the band Living Colour, founded the Black Rock Coalition (BRC), along with journalist Greg Tate and music producer Konda Mason. The BRC was founded to help promote African American rock artists because mainstream record companies were not doing an adequate job. In fact, in the mid '80s when "hair metal" was the most popular flavor of rock, black artists were all but ignored because they did not fit the image that record companies were trying to promote in the rock world. Rap music, which had been steadily gaining momentum in the industry since the late '70s, was the style that record companies were promoting. African American artists almost exclusively created the most popular rap music in the mid '80s, and this was the only kind of music by black artists that record companies advertised. They did not know what to do with a band like Living Colour—a virtuosic rock band comprised of four African Americans. Thankfully, for us fans, Living Colour is one of the rare examples of a band that broke through the race barrier and was able to get some radio play.

According to the organization's website, "the BRC opposes those racist and reactionary forces within the American music industry which undermine and purloin our musical legacy and deny Black artists the expressive freedom and economic rewards that our Caucasian counterparts enjoy as a matter of course."[20] There is no doubt that racism has played a disturbing role in rock music in

[20] http://www.blackrockcoalition.org/

many ways—from ignoring black artists to literally stealing music from them. As an example of the latter, Vincent Miller describes how the recording artist Moby sampled from a 1959 Alan Lomax recording of African American singer Vera Hall on his song "Natural Blues." This could be viewed as a tip of the musical hat to an earlier artist to raise awareness about her and cite her as an influence. But, regardless of intent, Miller points out: "The work continues the long history of white artists and producers profiting more from the work of black artists than do the artists themselves."[21] Miller goes on to explain that the song "Natural Blues" was later used in a Calvin Klein ad campaign, undoubtedly bringing in a hefty sum to both the company and Moby.

The title of this section is borrowed from a documentary called *Electric Purgatory: The Fate of the Black Rocker* (Payback Productions, 2008). The film showcases dozens of African American rock artists, many of whom mainstream radio ignores, and does an excellent job of setting up the historical context from which rock music emerged out of the black community. African American rock artists continue to push the musical envelope and integrate a variety of musical styles into their work, often in the face of an industry that does not care about them. During one part of the film, Doug Pinnick, lead singer and bassist for the band King's X, passionately describes how his band was hailed as one of the best acts at Woodstock '94 by

[21] Miller, 74.

several high-profile critics, but that praise did not result in any record sales. King's X is a trio and two of the members are Caucasian, but Pinnick is the front man and sets the tone for the rest of the band. Rock fans uneasy with an African American taking such a prominent role in a rock band are allowing racist attitudes (even subtle ones) to affect their listening habits.

As a fan of King's X, I have seen the band numerous times. The last time I saw them happened to fall on a day immediately after the death of Michael Jackson. The Motown Museum in Detroit was holding a candlelight service in his honor, so on my way home from the King's X show, I stopped by to check it out. I was moved to write an entry for *America* magazine's In All Things blog about some musings rolling around in my head regarding race and rock:

> Yesterday I attended a concert performed by the band King's X, a favorite of mine for over 15 years. I have seen the band at least a dozen times and they never disappoint. King's X is a hard rock band comprised of three very accomplished musicians. Their sound has been described as the "Beatles meets AC/DC" because their crunchy guitars and driving rhythm section are accompanied by impressive three part harmonies. I attend a lot of hard rock shows, and when I look around at the audience at most of these venues I notice a lot of people similar to me—namely white and male. Granted, I've noticed more females appearing at shows in the last 5 years or so, some of whom are dragged by their boyfriends/husbands. But rarely do I see African Americans at hard rock shows. King's X is an exception. Doug Pinnick, the lead singer and bass player, is African

American. Whether it is this fact alone, or Pinnick's preacher-like style of singing, King's X attracts a handful (or more) of African American fans to their live performances. Last night was no exception. I noticed some black faces amidst a sea of mostly white ones, including one blind African American woman who seemed to be in a mystical state during the entire show.

Driving home to my apartment in Detroit, I cruised down West Grand Blvd. to the original home of Motown Records, dubbed "Hitsville USA." Over 3,000 people had gathered in front of the old recording studio to pay homage to Michael Jackson with a candlelight vigil. I spent some time looking over the crowd. African Americans and whites mingled, sharing their memories and love for a pop culture icon. Knowing that the city is about 85% African American, I imagined that most of the white faces commuted in from the suburbs to pay tribute to the "King of Pop" who recorded a number of hits with his brothers in the Jackson 5 in Studio A at Motown Records. By the time the Jackson 5 were generating hits in the late 60's, blacks and whites alike enjoyed Motown music. Somehow its appeal was able to transcend race.

Today rock and roll is, sadly, very segregated. Given that rock music rose from the Blues and its foundation in black slave culture, this separation is especially sad. What could be a bridge between races, namely rock music, is often ignored, either through societal pressure to conform to what is considered "black" or "white" in popular culture, or perhaps due to how music is marketed (or both). Some music artists, such as King's X and Michael Jackson, breach the boundaries between "black" and "white" music. Popular music fans have witnessed white audiences growing more familiar with hip-hop artists, and some white hip-hop artists have even become stars of the genre. (Late last year, Vibe magazine readers voted the white hip-hop performer Eminem the best living rapper.) It may be a cliché, but music can and does bring people together—people who would not normally socialize with one another. This is, I believe, a positive event. I look forward to the day when I peruse the audience at a hard rock show and realize that I am in the racial minority.[22]

Issues of race are never easy to discuss. Better to ignore them, we believe, than to open that can of worms and risk hurting others' feelings and perhaps having our own feelings hurt. But if we do not discuss these issues, they will fester, which will result in animosity and greater suffering. Father Bryan Massingale, who teaches theology at Marquette University, holds an interesting role as an African American priest in a primarily white U.S. Roman Catholic Church. Father Massingale states that, for even the most well-meaning white folks, he becomes "a living 'ink blot' upon which they (white people) read their own unexamined concerns, fears, and anxieties."[23] It is only when people

[22] http://www.americamagazine.org/blog/blog.cfm?blog_id=2&category_id=68518090-3048-741E-3875600486118345. Reprinted with permission of America Press, Inc. © 2009. All rights reserved. For subscription information, call 1-800-627-9533 or visit www.america magazine.org.

[23] Bryan Massingale, "Race, racism engage us at a gut level," *National Catholic Reporter* (April 4, 2008), http://ncronline.org/node/558.

live, work, play music with, and talk to others who are different from them that a more realistic and truthful understanding emerges. According to Catholic social teaching, racism is a "social sin." This means that even if we as individuals make choices to avoid racist thoughts and actions, we are necessarily a part of a society that, as a whole, promotes discrimination. Whites benefit in a culture that marginalizes blacks. As the BRC pointed out in their mission statement, white rock musicians enjoy a level of artistic and financial success that has eluded African American rock musicians. Could it be that white rock musicians and fans, as Fr. Massingale suggests, are reading their own fears and anxieties onto black rock musicians?

It might be a valuable exercise for white rock fans and musicians reading this to look at their assumptions about race and rock music. When you see a black rock group performing (or a band with a couple of African Americans along with musicians of other races), what assumptions do you bring to the experience? What emotions and images are conjured when you listen to such groups? One cannot investigate the history of rock and roll music without listening to literally hundreds, if not thousands, of African American rockers. By delving into the history of rock and roll music, white fans might grow in their appreciation for the African American contributions to the music they love. And finally, listening to contemporary bands (and purchasing their music), perhaps some listed on the BRC website, could be a rock-style sign of solidarity as well as a rock spiritual/social justice exercise.

After having investigated intersections of theology, spirituality, and social justice with rock music, I am now going to present some concrete examples of how I understand these intersections to manifest themselves in our contemporary world. The next chapter is a collection of six short essays I wrote, along with some introductory comments. Reprinting these essays is my attempt to move from the more theoretical base of the other chapters and show how I search for the divine in rock music and culture. It will, I pray, encourage readers to reflect on how they engage in this search as well.

Chapter 5

Bringing Rock to the Table

Finding connections between rock music and religion is not always easy. As I stated previously, performing an exegetical analysis of rock music lyrics can be somewhat useful but it is only one way to build this bridge. Discovering new ways to bring these two powerful phenomena together has been a pursuit of mine for a number of years. I cannot claim to have figured out the ideal ways to integrate rock music and religion/spirituality/theology, but I have been able to contemplate on this topic and draw a few tentative conclusions. I consider this endeavor one that will last the rest of my life—as both rock fan and amateur theologian—so even these "conclusions" are open to critique and change. In many ways this is similar to our sense of spirituality, an aspect of our earthly life that can continue to evolve until we die. As soon as we think we have our spiritual life figured out, something throws dissonance into our interior composition and we

114

are left staring at a jumble of ragged notes rather than a complete oeuvre.

So, how *do* you juxtapose rock music and religion in an intelligent, powerful, and descriptive way, even if it is tentative? The blog rockandtheology.com is one excellent resource to examine. Most of the writers are professional theologians as well as amateur (or better) rock musicians. Their writers' musings have provided me with much intellectual consolation as well as challenged some of my assumptions about this topic. The rest of this chapter holds examples of my own thinking on rock and religion—and all of the multiple layers of meaning contained in those two words. Most of these short essays were published previously online, either at bustedhalo.com or in *America* magazine (in either print form or on the website americamagazine.org). I hope this chapter provides some insights into how I juggle rock music and theology, but also encourages the reader to examine his or her own thinking and prayer about how to be an authentic person in the not-too-dissimilar worlds of rock and religion.

Aimee Mann

When I was studying philosophy at Loyola University in Chicago, I started writing CD reviews for a local college paper. I learned a lot about writing music reviews—the innate style of the music review, what I liked and did not like included in a review, and how to describe an album while also upholding a sense of mystery about the music for the reader. Music reviews should not be pontifications about the reviewer's personal tastes—certainly personal taste will come into play, but communicating it is not the ultimate goal. Being a music reviewer is to be a steward of an artist's creative product. Whether criticizing or praising an album, the reviewer has to remember that the motivation to create music transcends the musician. This should give the reviewer pause and encourage her to tread lightly on another's soulful expression of the creative force that is greater than any of us.

I have been an Aimee Mann fan since she released her second solo album, *I'm With Stupid*, in the mid '90s. So when I heard she was going to release a new album in 2005, and a concept album at that, I jumped at the chance to review it for an online magazine for "spiritual seekers" called *Busted Halo*. As I listened to the lyrics, theme, and mood of the songs, the book *Addiction and Grace* by physician and spiritual writer Gerald May occurred to me. I wondered what would happen if I listened to the album with the themes of that book (at least how I understood and integrated them) as a lens for interpretation? The following is my attempt to do this.

"The Forgotten Arm:
Aimee Mann's new album is a knockout"[1]

> *Addiction and Grace*, the title of a Christian spiritual classic by Gerald May, is also an apt description for Aimee Mann's latest disc, *The Forgotten Arm*. Her new collection of songs

[1] A version of this article originally appeared on bustedhalo.com. Reprinted with permission. © 2005. All rights reserved.

marks the fifth solo release for the former 'til Tuesday front woman and bassist, and marks the first time she has dared to tread into the highly dangerous territory known as "The Concept Album." Fear not, music fans, *The Forgotten Arm* is a musical novella that contains some of Mann's finest work to date.

Mann's musical and lyrical arc recounts the story of John—a drug addict—and Caroline who meet at the Virginia State Fair in the 70's and begin a troubled journey across the U.S. Through her melodies Mann is able to evoke in the listener a mood that perfectly reflects her characters' often-desperate condition. Ultimately, however, she rescues these characters with a gleam of hope in the redeeming power of love.

"The King of the Jailhouse," sets the tone for John and Caroline's troubling co-dependent relationship. These lovers are drawn together with a desire to share their distressed lives, believing that by sharing their burdens they will lighten their load. Their pain, physical and emotional, swirls together as the couple, each desperate for love, begin to realize that their problems are not as easy to bear as they had assumed. John is a boxer, but he spends most of his time fighting himself and the cycle of addiction and depression that grips him. For her part, Caroline begins to see the poignant truth of his life and desperately tries to keep her lover clean, all the while knowing that she alone cannot do it.

Mann has created very realistic characters and puts them in an all-too-real troubled relationship. As a child of the 70's, it is not a coincidence that Mann set her story in this decade and that she focuses on the casual attitude that many held about the drug culture. Mann digs into the underbelly of this culture and she is not afraid to show the sometimes-sad consequences of embracing it. John knows that there is something wrong with him, but is unable to understand the root of his problems. Listeners are left to wonder throughout the album if Caroline's love will ultimately help John to escape the vice-like grip of his addictions. While Mann ultimately provides no certain answer, she leaves room for hope.

Few contemporary songwriters can struggle with complex themes like grace, pain, love, desolation, and redemption as expertly as Mann. In a musical landscape filled with superficiality, she is one of the few ambassadors of intelligent, melodic music. Mann has repeatedly proven herself a master of setting the story of distressing relationships to music. Many of her previous solo albums focus at least partly on this theme, but *The Forgotten Arm* is her most overt attempt to grapple with the pain two human beings can inflict upon one another in a relationship, whether intended or not. The title, *The Forgotten Arm*, refers to a concept in boxing—one of Mann's favorite hobbies. If a boxer repeatedly delivers blows with his left arm, his opponent will focus all of his attention on blocking the punches from the left, leaving him open for a surprise uppercut from the "forgotten" right arm.

The painful surprises, multiple broken promises and broken hearts become the "forgotten arm" in John and Caroline's relationship. But this is not the whole story. Toward the end of Mann's musical tale, John begins to understand and regret the effect his decisions are having on Caroline and their relationship. The album's last song, "Beautiful" is a hauntingly gorgeous testimony to the ability some possess to see beauty even in a troubled relationship. In it, Caroline wonders if John will ever see himself the way she does—as a troubled but beautiful human being. Certainly, one need not struggle with addiction to resonate with that sentiment.

Syd Barrett

While Syd Barrett did not release a lot of music in his lifetime, he definitely gained cult status in the rock world, primarily due to his association with the band Pink Floyd. Barrett was a founding member of this progressive rock band in the late '60s and was responsible for a number of compositions on their first album, *Piper at the Gates of Dawn*. Barrett's tenure in the band was short—guitarist David Gilmour ultimately replaced him—but his legacy in the band continued. Floyd's 1975 masterwork, *Shine on You Crazy Diamond*, a nine-part composition from the album *Wish You Were Here*, was written as a tribute to Syd Barrett. The title says it all: Barrett was brilliant and multifaceted like a diamond, but he struggled with obvious mental problems that pursued him until his death at age sixty in 2007.

The occasion of Barrett's death got me thinking. I pulled out my copy of *Piper* and reveled in Barrett's quirky lyrics and the sometimes carnival-like feel of his compositions. Barrett was a mad genius. It occurred to me, from my knowledge of the lives of the saints, that some of the women and men whom the Catholic Church revered as "holy" were also not exactly psychologically normal by contemporary DSM-IV standards! Some saw visions and heard God speaking to them; others lived overly ascetic lives and put their bodies and minds through incredible strains. And yet, we look up to these women and men as examples of the holy life. Sometimes there is a thin veil between genius (or holiness) and what we perceive as "abnormal" behavior. And maybe that is just fine!

"Shine on: Syd Barrett and the Saints"[2]

Syd Barrett, cofounder of the legendary rock band Pink Floyd, recently passed away at the age of 60. Barrett was a troubled soul, an amalgamation of genius and lunacy who, in the 60's, ingested LSD like Pez candy and wrote narcotic-inspired songs that eventually influenced thousands of musicians. Barrett's tenure in Pink Floyd was short—he lasted only one album after which his band mates dismissed him for his crazy, erratic behavior, and replaced him with guitarist and vocalist David Gilmour. Syd spent the past 3 decades living in anonymity in England, avoiding the press and staying far away from the music business.

Despite, or perhaps due to his quasi-monastic seclusion, many rock bands continued to cite Barrett as an influence decades after writing his last song. I recall first hearing about Barrett from one of my first band mates in the late 80's. He invited me to listen to Floyd's first album, *The Piper at the Gates of Dawn* in his dorm room. The whimsical but catchy song "Bike" blasted out of his stereo speakers, shaking the dormitory walls. The song impressed me for quite some time—I can still recall its melody and quirky lyrics. Almost a dozen years later, a band I played with in Chicago

[2] A version of this article originally appeared on bustedhalo.com. Reprinted with permission. © 2006. All rights reserved.

covered Barrett's tune, "Matilda Mother," another track from *Piper*. Barrett's music, similar to that of cult favorites The Velvet Underground, never sold well, but, as one music critic exaggeratedly quipped, everyone who bought a copy started a band.

To be honest, what intrigued me about Syd Barrett was not so much the bizarre chord progressions in his songs, it was his strange behavior and the near-mythic stories that emerged about him. I heard stories from fellow musicians —I have subsequently dubbed them "musical legends" very akin to the "urban legend" stories that teenagers trade during sleepover parties. Barrett's LSD use, some claimed, brought his mind to a place beyond genius and into lunacy. This is why he spent time interned in a sanitarium—he saw what human beings should never see. Did he see God? Did he have a vision that altered his perception forever or was he simply a unique variation on the sad "live fast, die young, leave a beautiful corpse" cliché: live fast, die old(er) and hold a private funeral? Who knows? I admit that I was fascinated by these musical legends, and what's more, I believed I could discern a kernel of truth within them.

In his Autobiography, Ignatius Loyola describes a vision he had of three musical notes that he discerned symbolized the Trinity. St. Teresa of Avila experienced, "Intellectual visions and locutions," according to the *New Advent Catholic Encyclopedia*. Often, these fascinating experiences of the divine are what attract people to the saints. When it comes to saints' life activities, going to mass daily never holds the same panache as kissing a leper's sores, bi-locating, or hearing the Virgin Mary deliver a message to the world. These instances of strange behaviors are attractive to us—they are far from ordinary and most of us will never experience anything close to them. Some of their contemporaries assumed that many of these saints were insane. Apologists, however, proclaim that their bizarre visions and behavior were the result of their hearts and minds being totally infused with God's love.

Who is correct? Could it be that both parties have a partial grasp of the truth? The ambiguous and narrow space between holiness, genius and insanity is a place where all of these figures, Barrett included, find common ground. Is it not possible that God could work through a person's mental illness, bizarre actions, or alleged visions? Millions of people flock to Marian apparition sites every year, yet only a small minority has reported actually seeing the Virgin Mary appear. Whether or not these are "legit" visions is an issue about which not even the Catholic Church has given a final word. What cannot be denied, however, is that millions of faithful people have found strength, grace, and have come closer to God as a result of these devotions.

I am not claiming that Syd Barrett is a contemporary saint. But why have Barrett's music and life remained so attractive years after he disappeared from the public eye? There's no doubt that, despite his faults and addictions, Barrett left an indelible mark on rock and roll music and influenced generations of listeners and musicians with his creative writing and beguiling guitar playing. His music was his gift to the world, and just perhaps, it was also the way God worked through him.

Slayer

Heavy metal may be the most despised form of rock music. Even many die-hard rock fans do not like it. There are several possible explanations for this. First of all, some of the imagery can seem silly—common themes include demons, dungeons and dragons, immature sexual innuendos, and, well, that is about it! At least some detractors of heavy metal believe it is attractive to only Neanderthals. I consider myself a fairly intelligent guy and I enjoy a lot of heavy metal bands. The music is very powerful and aggressive—two words that no one would use to describe me! So perhaps metal taps into my inner spiritual energy that longs to be released. Whatever the reason, I find some metal music to be invigorating and even deeply profound.

Many readers might know that the term "heavy metal" is a term that describes dozens of styles of music. There is hair metal, death metal, black metal, doom metal, thrash metal, progressive metal, speed metal, and several more. Each of these, believe it or not, has a distinct musical form. The band Slayer, for example, is considered thrash metal. According to Wikipedia, "Slayer's musical traits involve fast tremolo picking, atonal guitar solos, double bass drumming, and shouting vocals."[3] In short, the music is brutal. I held a cursory interest in Slayer since they were considered one of the founding thrash metal bands. A few years back, during the height of the Iraq war, when Slayer released an album called *Christ Illusion* that was favorably reviewed in the *New York Times*, I decided to purchase it and listen carefully to what I had all but ignored for several years. What I found surprised me.

[3] http://en.wikipedia.org/wiki/Slayer

"Christ Illusion: *Slayer's new album confronts America's religious hypocrisy*"[4]

In recent years I have found that I do not recognize many names on the Billboard music charts. Perhaps this is a sign that I am getting older and less connected to what is "hot" right now, but—to borrow a line from the movie *This is Spinal Tap*—I prefer to think that my musical tastes have gotten a bit more "selective."

In either case, I was very surprised recently to see a familiar and controversial name at the top of the charts. The thrash metal band Slayer had sold enough units of their new disc, *Christ Illusion* (over 60,000 in the first week) to break into the top five. The CD, Slayer's first in five years, was favorably reviewed in numerous national newspapers, including the *New York Times*. How did an underground extreme heavy metal band that prides itself on songs about Satan become so respectable? The answer should be of interest to all spiritual seekers.

The cover for *Christ Illusion* is, to say the least, shocking. A Christ figure, bruised and beaten, wearing a crown of thorns, stands in a vile pool of blood and death, with the decapitated heads of several people floating around him and war raging on all sides. One of the heads appears to be that of soon-to-be-saint Mother Teresa. On the figure's chest is a tattoo of a variation of the Sacred Heart and the word "jihad" written above it. Not exactly my first choice for a photo on my annual Christmas card.

---

[4] A version of this article originally appeared on bustedhalo.com. Reprinted with permission. © 2006. All rights reserved.

When I first glanced at the cover, my eyes were immediately drawn to the Christ figure's arms—they are cut off at the elbow, leaving him looking all the more pathetic and helpless. I thought of the prayer by St. Theresa of Avilla—Lord Christ, You have no body on earth but ours, *No hands but ours, No feet but ours . . .* The point of this prayer is that Jesus is no longer with us in physical form, so it is up to his followers to continue his work; this has been the Christian mission for 2,000 years. Slayer's graphic and grotesque cover art takes St. Theresa's prayer, flips it around and kicks it a few times in the stomach.

A cursory listen to the album reveals songs that express Slayer's disgust with religious hypocrisy. The Christian community has failed to continue Christ's work on earth, and additionally, has used the faith to, in effect, rip his arms off again and again by justifying war and violence in His name. The word "jihad" tattooed to the Christ figure's chest on the cover illustration is very telling. The United States, a Christian nation, "under God and indivisible," is conducting its own "holy war" in the Middle East, allowing torture of prisoners of war and supporting foreign policies that are the antithesis of true Christian teaching.

One does not normally look to heavy metal (and especially a band like Slayer) for political commentary, but given the popularity of their new release, it seems that Slayer has struck a chord with many music fans. One review called *Christ Illusion* the most political record of the year after Neil Young's most recent release, *Living with War*.

The members of Slayer have never been religious apologists, so their recent offering is pretty typical of what they have done for the past 20 years. They have no use for Christianity or any organized religion. The difference now is that tens of thousands of music fans are taking notice, and are angry enough about what they see in politics and organized religion to catapult the band and its acerbic social commentary to the top of the music charts. Christians could easily ignore Slayer—and many have for over two decades. Christians could also blacklist the band's music and even speak out against it in public. This not only would be ill-advised, it would also miss the point.

Instead, the question Christians should ask themselves is "Why are so many people interested in what this band is communicating?" A bit of collective introspection on what Christians are supporting in the name of Jesus could be a better response. Is our country, as Slayer wants to suggest, supporting our own brand of "jihad" through an unjust war in Iraq and the global war on terror we have initiated? If there is one point on which the world's major religions agree it is that violence has no rational place with faith. How ironic that our society needs a band that creates such aggressive music to teach us this.

Does Madonna Belong in the Rock and Roll Hall of Fame?[5]

As you read this, someone in Cleveland at the Rock and Roll Hall of Fame Museum is very likely admiring Madonna's exhibit. Does this bother anyone besides me?! I have been accused on many occasions of being a "music snob" but, while I surely need to own up to my tendencies toward musical elitism, it seems to me that common sense

[5] Previously unpublished.

dictates that inducting Madonna into a museum that celebrates rock and roll was a bad idea.

Many rock fans were disgusted by this development. How could Madonna make the cut, they wonder, and be placed alongside the pantheon of rock royalty who have shaped the most popular and influential music of the twentieth century? Janis Joplin, Hendrix, the Beatles, the Stones, The Who, Dylan, and . . . Madonna?! These critics may have a point, and the outcry raises an important question. What does it mean for someone and her music to be considered "rock and roll"?

This situation is not unlike the Vatican's recent promulgation about tightening up the canonization process. Both cases center on the notion of authenticity and credibility. In the case of Catholic sainthood, the unprecedented numbers of women and men that John Paul II beatified and canonized staggered even his staunch supporters. Recent allegations that "sainthood" was losing its meaning in the popular forum likely led the Vatican to declare that, while it was not changing the canonization process, its governing rules would be followed more strictly. Writing in the March 10th issue, the editors of *America* magazine observed, "Rumors of laxity in the canonization process only raise doubts among Catholics over whether certain candidates truly deserve the title 'saint.'"

Echoes of this attitude can be found throughout the rock and roll journalism of the past thirty plus years. Using heavy metal as an example, Robert Walser, in his book *Running with the Devil: Power, Gender and Madness in Heavy*

Metal Music, explains that rock journalists and critics despised many of the popular heavy metal bands of the early '70s like Kiss and Alice Cooper solely because too many people liked them. He writes, "Flushed with enthusiasm for the artistic importance of rock music, critics were deeply suspicious of commercially successful music, which smacked of 'sell-out' because it appealed to too many people."[6] Could the Vatican and rock critics be onto something here? Are some "saints" and "rockers," to borrow from the punk lexicon, only posers?

Whether or not Madonna deserves to be in the Rock and Roll Hall of Fame has been debated in the press since the nominees were announced. She joins the likes of John Mellencamp, The Ventures, and Leonard Cohen as this year's Hall class. I am not interested in trying to bash or praise Madonna. The negative reaction of so many rock fans and critics, however, is something I find fascinating. It implies that there is something that they/we believe can legitimately be labeled "rock music" and that Madonna falls well outside of its boundaries. Madonna has been called too "polished" to be rock and roll. She is all about image over music, many say. She has not paid her dues by playing in dingy clubs, something she could not have done anyway since she does not really play an instrument—yet another blow against her rock credibility.

---

[6] Robert Walser, *Running with the Devil: Power, Gender and Madness in Heavy Metal Music* (Middletown: Wesleyan University Press, 1993), 10–11.

Many Catholics, if recent reports are to be believed, have looked askance at the exponential growth in the communion of saints during the John Paul II pontificate. Were some canonizations, some wonder, just the result of political maneuvering? In his recent Op-Ed piece in the *New York Times* about the Vatican's statement regarding sainthood, Fr. Jim Martin, SJ, writes, "Candidates (for sainthood) should not be promoted by small interest groups."[7] In other words, the appeal of a particular candidate for sainthood needs to exceed well beyond the borders of a community or even a country. There must be some criteria with which to judge the worthiness of holding the title "saint," otherwise it loses its vital meaning.

Perhaps the lesson to be learned is that, as much as we need saints—both religious and secular—we also crave authenticity. We do not desire saints for their own sake, but rather because they serve as examples of something sacred and unique. We want to know that the people for whom we hold devotions are the "real deal." The controversies surrounding Madonna's induction and the recent Vatican statement are, I believe, healthy indications that we have not lost sight of this.

Perhaps as an ironic gesture, or more likely as an answer to her critics, Madonna asked punk pioneers and fellow Michiganders the Stooges to perform two of her songs at the Rock and Roll Hall of Fame induction ceremony. The

[7] James Martin, SJ, "Trials of the Saints," *New York Times* Op-Ed page (March 3, 2008).

Stooges are fronted by Iggy Pop, a man who embodies the rock and roll ethos better than just about anyone else. The Stooges are considered exceptionally influential in the rock and roll world, yet they have never been inducted into the Hall of Fame.[8] Clearly, by giving a nod to these rock pioneers, it seems that even Madonna understands the importance of credibility if the Rock and Roll Hall of Fame is going to mean anything significant to anyone. I believe Vatican officials would nod approvingly at this sentiment.

Motown

In recent years, I have focused more of my writing on the city of Detroit. I love the city. My wife and I are both from inner-ring suburbs but we are choosing to live and raise a family in the city of Detroit. This comes with its fair share of blessings and challenges, as any decision does.

One of the blessings of living in Detroit is discovering about the city's history, almost on a daily basis. There is a rich history in Detroit—not only about the auto industry but the arts, music, and architecture as well. Last year marked the fiftieth anniversary of Motown Records, founded in Detroit by Berry Gordy Jr. As a child of Detroit, Gordy was very familiar with the automobile industry and he modeled important aspects of his music business on the automobile business, specifically, Henry Ford's style of running an automobile business.

---

[8] The Stooges were finally inducted into the Rock and Roll Hall of Fame two years after I wrote this piece.

Since Ford's workforce was comprised primarily of immigrants, he started schools to teach his workers the English language and the American way of life. These "Americanization" schools were not uncontroversial. One of the goals was to "standardize" immigrants so that they acted and spoke like Americans "should," at least according to Ford. But who can claim to set the standard for what being an American actually entails? Gordy picked up on this idea when he initiated his "finishing" school at Motown Records to teach mostly poor young African American kids how to look and act refined (read: white). Gordy was a complicated man, which is one reason I find him so fascinating.

To help mark the fiftieth anniversary of Motown Records, I wrote the following article for *America* magazine. It showcases Motown's thirst for and activism toward social justice, as well as the ambiguities of what it takes to run a large record company.

"That Motown Sound: Berry Gordy, Jr. and the African-American experience"[9]

> Throughout 2009 Motown Records celebrates its 50th anniversary with a series of special events and performances that kicked off January 12. Motown's extraordinary accomplishments include an unprecedented 63 number-one hit songs from 1961 to 1971 by artists that make up a Mt.

[9] Reprinted with permission of America Press, Inc. © 2009. All rights reserved. For subscription information, call 1-800-627-9533 or visit www.americamagazine.org.

Rushmore of pop music: Smokey Robinson, Marvin Gaye, The Supremes, The Temptations, Martha and the Vandellas and The Four Tops, among many others.

The music Motown created, which symbolizes coming of age, celebration, and spiritual awakening, is timeless and means so much to so many people. Motown placed African Americans firmly in the pop music pantheon and created a unique sound that appealed to people of all races.

In 1959 Berry Gordy Jr. started Motown Records with an $800 loan from his family. Four years after Brown v. Board of Education cleared the way for racial integration and four years prior to Martin Luther King's "I Have a Dream" speech, an African American initiated a pop music revolution in the United States. He modeled Motown Records on the automobile assembly line he had worked on earlier in his life. He aimed to turn out hit songs, create top of the line artists, and present a polished image that could be marketed to a general audience. Gordy recruited several songwriters to help churn out records. The most famous team was Holland-Dozier-Holland who penned dozens of popular songs for Motown including "Please Mr. Postman," "Where Did Our Love Go?" and "How Sweet It Is (To Be Loved By You)." Gordy's model succeeded and Motown became the first "Hit Factory."

Motown was more than a music studio, however. It was also a school for the singer-performers, many of whom were local teenagers from less privileged backgrounds. Diana Ross, for example, lived in Detroit's Brewster-Douglass Projects before getting her big break with Motown. Gordy employed instructors to help his performers choreograph their acts, and to teach them proper poise and etiquette. The record company drew heavy criticism, however, for what some believed was a disgraceful practice of making black singers palatable to a white audience. During the 1967 Detroit riots, Motown Records received a number of threatening phone calls.

The success of Motown was due in large part to what is referred to as the "Motown Sound," which flowed from three sources. First, the Funk Brothers, the Motown house band, made a major contribution to this unique sound. These musicians performed on most of the Motown hits from 1959 to the early 1970s, but, unjustly, were seldom credited on the album covers. The Funk Brothers were incredible musicians and were responsible for the consistency and groove of the Motown Sound.

The second feature of the Motown Sound was the primitive but effective method of generating a "reverb" that helped make some Motown songs sound like they were recorded live on stage. The music and vocals were broadcast from the famous Studio A at Motown headquarters on West Grand Boulevard to the attic of the building (known as the echo chamber) through a hole cut in the ceiling. The sound bounced around in the vacant space, was picked up by a microphone, and then recorded. During a time before synthesizers and computerized recording, this was an ingenious method of creating a unique sound.

Third, the performers also made liberal use of the tambourine. Black church gospel choirs often played a tambourine to keep the dynamic rhythm steady and excite a congregation. The tambourine was simple to play, easy to record in the studio, and, as it turned out, more pleasing to the ear when the music was played on small transistor radios, which were popular during Motown's peak years.

Motown Records served an important role in the civil rights struggles of the 1960s. Their "Spoken Word" series held the exclusive right to record the speeches of Martin

Luther King, Jr. In June, 1963, two months before the March on Washington, Motown recorded King's "I Have a Dream" speech as he delivered it in Detroit.

The company was also an active participant in the improvement of the city of Detroit, and it hired local African Americans for prominent jobs. As the leader of the largest black-owned business in the country, Berry Gordy himself was a role model for young African Americans, which was no small thing at the time.

In addition to its fun, bouncy hits, Motown also produced socially conscious pop music. Marvin Gaye's classic 1971 album "What's Going On," one of the last Motown albums recorded in Detroit before the company moved to Los Angeles, is a perfect example of music that shines a light on justice issues like inner-city poverty, racism, war, environmentalism and drug abuse.

While Berry Gordy initially opposed Gaye's desire to record this album because of the serious nature of the lyrics, Gordy eventually conceded. It became one of the biggest selling Motown albums of all time. The title song also paved the way for later artists to highlight social concerns. Contemporary rock, soul and R&B artists of all races still cite "What's Going On" as a major influence.

While the music of Motown did not change race relations either quickly or single-handedly, of course, it was the first popular music in the United States marketed to people of many races. Ironically, many today note the joy and innocence associated with the music, but the back story is that during a disgraceful time in U.S. history, when blacks were being beaten on the streets of urban America, Motown stars were performing to the delight of white audiences, slowly chipping away at racist attitudes. In this anniversary year, fans are celebrating the music of Motown—and more than that. For its fans, Motown also became a symbol of hope.

Bruce Springsteen

No one puts on a rock concert like Bruce Springsteen! All the elements are present: loud and crunchy guitars, a tight rhythm section, wailing organ and keyboards, and a sense of showmanship that is unparalleled in the music business today. There is no separation between performer and audience. A Springsteen show truly is a spiritual experience. After leaving a Springsteen show, as Tom Massaro, SJ, commented on the *America* magazine blog, "concert-goers come away transformed, having experienced nothing less than a profound liturgical experience."

When I last saw Springsteen perform live in November of 2009, I knew I had to put the experience in writing. But what can one express that has not already been written? There are several volumes published about Springsteen's Catholic imagination, the sociological import of his music, and analyses regarding what he means to the American psyche. What could I possibly contribute to the mountain of work already out there about the Boss? Then it occurred to me—why not write about how *fun* it is to see Springsteen in concert?!

Unalloyed joy is all too infrequent in our lives. Perhaps your wedding day or the birth of your first child are examples of such an emotive experience. But a Springsteen show is also one such example. His shows are invigorating and overflowing with joy—they are excursions into the marrow of life. I decided to write about this aspect of a Springsteen show. I have so much fun at his shows and they make me authentically happy—and while that is not incredibly profound (at least not on an intellectual basis), it is truth.

"Proving It All Night:
Bruce Springsteen plays the Motor City"[10]

> Some call Bruce Springsteen "The Boss" but on November 13, during a performance with the E Street Band in Detroit, he was working for the audience. (His national tour ended in Buffalo on Nov. 22.) The third song of the almost three-hour set, an energy-infused version of "Johnny 99" from the "Nebraska" album, could not have been more poignant, with its description of auto plants closing and the desperation that attends an economic recession. While many in the Detroit audience were likely feeling the pinch of these hard times, Springsteen paused to solicit help for a popular local non-profit, Focus Hope. This grand gesture reminded the crowd that there are those who barely scrape by, even during times of plenty, and who could never afford to attend one of his shows.
>
> Many distinguished scholars have written about Springsteen, from Andrew Greeley's discussion of his

"Catholic imagination" to Robert Coles' collected testimonials on what average Americans feel about his songs. What makes a Springsteen show great is the way it serves as a clarion call to wake up, embrace life and have fun! This is not musical escapism—no one is denying the suffering felt by so many, least of all Springsteen, who has been writing about the plight of the average worker for three decades. But he has a striking ability to make a 20,000-seat arena feel intimate, as though the show were meant for each individual present. The Boss is on a mission: to give the audience three hours of enjoyment and the permission to forget the depressing news headlines.

Springsteen has experienced a creative renaissance since 9/11, when he felt compelled to write new material in response to the national tragedy. Ever since, he has attempted to snap us out of our anger, desire for revenge and the general malaise brought on by a bad economy.

Springsteen suffered some geographical disorientation at the beginning of the show in Detroit, shouting "Hello Ohio!" to the crowd multiple times before his longtime sideman and guitarist Steve Van Zandt reminded him where he was playing. Apologetic, he quickly made up for the gaffe by playing local-audience favorites, including Bob Seger's "Ramblin' Gamblin' Man" and the fun set-list staple, "Detroit Medley." After this, all was forgiven and the audience fed the band the burst of adrenaline it needed for its performance to explode.

This was my seventh Springsteen concert since 1988 and I can say that the energy level of the performances has never decreased. Springsteen exhibits few signs that he is a 60-year-old man. He wears a small brace on his right hand, most likely to stave off developing carpal-tunnel syndrome from years of pounding on guitar strings with unbridled fury. If you have ever seen a Springsteen show up close, you know how much of himself he spills onto the stage. He frequently spits to clear his throat, and after about six songs there is a steady stream of sweat dripping off of his arms and fingers. After the show a roadie must have to mop up the evidence of Springsteen's physical sacrifice for his fans.

Bruce does not save himself simply for big venues like Madison Square Garden. He pours himself out as much in Des Moines as in New York City. He literally throws himself into the audience and surfs the crowd, trusting that they will carry him safely back to the stage. This is a connection that few entertainers can build, much less sustain for 35 years. He urges the crowd to take part in the festivities, allowing them to sing the first verse of "Hungry Heart" or the "Show a little faith" line in "Thunder Road." These moments are not contrived—they are tributes to songs that Springsteen realizes have transcended even him as author. They are not *his* songs, they are *our* songs, and that's all right with him.

While Springsteen never forgets that he is putting on a show, sometimes his performance can seem like an ego-building exercise. Yes, he is a selfless entertainer, giving all he has to the audience and pushing the E Street Band to do the same. Yet no one, including the band at times, knows what song is coming next. The Boss calls out songs at will and the band is expected to be ready to play—a display of command that Springsteen seems to relish.

For the last dozen shows or so on this recent tour Springsteen played some of his albums in their entirety. This was a gift to fans who have followed the band for decades, but it was also a tribute to the rock album as an art form at a time of digitized music when singles are consumed with little context. Listening to Bruce and band perform the album "Born to Run," one can hear how the songs blend into one another, musically and lyrically. The album is to be appreciated as a whole, not as a disparate collection of a few singles and some filler tunes. It was composed by a 20-something young man just coming into his own as a musician and a citizen of the world, wrestling with themes and questions that would infuse his songs for decades to come. It is part autobiography, part longing for love, part story of summers past and a desire for youth to continue forever.

The final song of the night was "Your Love Keeps Lifting Me Higher," made famous 40 years ago by Detroit crooner Jackie Wilson, and one Bruce has been playing often on this tour. The "your" in the title could refer to a lover, or to the audience, or to that which lifts our spirits when houses are foreclosing on our blocks, jobs are being lost and life dreams are being deferred. For me, it referred to Springsteen and the love he shows his fans. I left with my spirit feeling higher than it has in a long time.

Chapter 6

I AM FINDING WHO I AM

I suppose it is Randy's fault. Randy was my guitar teacher back in the early '80s when I had grandiose aspirations of being the next Eric Clapton or Jimmy Page. Actually, back then I wanted to be John Denver or Roger Whittaker, or one of the other folksy adult contemporary musicians my parents and their peers enjoyed. I ultimately quit playing guitar and took up the drums instead, but Randy's love for rock music inspired me and I am still feeling that inspiration today. Randy did not just teach kids how to play the guitar; he ran a "school of rock" twenty plus years before Jack Black's movie came along. Whenever I struggled with a chord progression, Randy would show me how to navigate the fret board on his acoustic, and then pull out an LP from his massive music library and say, "Check out how [*insert name of guitar god here*] pulls off this progression."

I heard the drop of the needle on vinyl, the anticipatory crackle, and then the aural nectar would flow into my ears! I knew even then that I would never be able to master the songs that Randy played for me from bands like Boston, Rush, Yes, Chicago, and Journey, but I did not really care. I was learning how to feed my soul and collect spiritual consolation from rock music. I have never stopped.

Around the time I was taking guitar lessons from Randy, I joined the Columbia Record and Tape Club by affixing a single copper penny to the subscription postcard I found in the Sunday morning paper. I recall the intensity of the adrenaline rush through my body as I studied the dozens of albums from which I could choose (all for only one cent!), trying not to drool all over the paper. Asia, Billy Squire, Devo, and Pat Benatar were, at the time, very popular artists and I desperately desired to hear their material, become a fan, and immerse myself completely into the world of rock music. When a box of cassettes appeared in the mailbox three weeks later, I savagely ripped it open and examined my newly acquired treasures. I removed each tape from its hermetically sealed plastic wrapping and held it up to my nose—that new music smell! I carefully placed one tape in my small radio/cassette player (purchased with my paper route money) and queued it to the beginning of the first song. Each cassette transported me out of myself and into a sweet musical destination.

At some point I realized that listening to the music was not enough—it was begging to be sung! There was a small space behind the outdoor air conditioner unit at our house where I would go in the summer with my cassette player and my cache of tapes. When the air turned on, the unit would create a din allowing me to sing along with the music without attracting an audience. I was able to keep this practice a secret until one day our neighbor commented that she enjoyed listening to me sing from their back patio. Self-conscious and embarrassed, I put an end to my nascent vocal career and brought my enjoyment back inside to the privacy of my bedroom. These two brief stories about my initial flirtations with rock music are part of my theo-musical autobiography, to which I now turn.

Theo-musical Autobiography

The inspiration for this chapter comes in part from theologian Clive Marsh's article "Theology as 'Soundtrack': Popular Culture and Narratives of the Self." This is an enlightening resource that I used in an earlier chapter, and I wish to return to one part of it here. Marsh declares that one role for theology vis-à-vis the arts in general—and rock music specifically—is to encourage churches to be safe realms where people can raise popular culture topics and explore their theological implications with others. This is not an opportunity, as Marsh insists, for churches to "offer 'Christian answers' to 'culture's questions.' "[1] Rather, such

[1] Clive Marsh, "Theology as 'Soundtrack': Popular Culture and Narratives of the Self," *Expository Times* 118.11 (2007): 541.

intercourse is meant for Christians to grapple with their/ our search for the interplay between faith and the culture in which we are all immersed. With this as a goal, I am referring to this chapter as my theo-musical autobiography. It is not a comprehensive life story, but a collection of snap-shots from my life as a fan of rock music and a rock musi-cian, and how these lived identities have helped me develop as a person of faith. I do not intend to offer Chris-tian answers to popular culture questions—I would much rather show how those questions have impacted my faith life and encouraged my rock and religion fandom.

In the introduction, I recounted my experience hearing the Detroit band The Romantics on a local rock radio station and feeling the desire to shout out at the chorus of their song "What I Like About You." The early '80s was a great time to be learning about rock music and listening to the radio. AC/DC, Van Halen, Rush, Led Zeppelin, and The Who were all played in heavy rotation. One local station initiated what they dubbed a D.R.E.A.D. club and gave out membership cards to listeners. D.R.E.A.D. stood for "Detroit Rockers Engaged in the Abolition of Disco." I surmised that to be a true rock fan one had to hate disco music—although at this point I doubt I knew much disco anyway. That did not stop me from sending away for the card, which I carried dutifully in my skinny wallet. I loved listening to the radio and I loved the feelings that accom-panied me when I heard rock blaring into my ears. The radio, during these early years of my rock fandom, became my comfort and my companion.

From the time I was in grade school, Sunday nights have been difficult for me. Anxiety builds constantly through the day in anticipation of the coming week with its unknown complications. Somehow, cutting through my usual preteen oblivion, I gained the insight that I could do certain things to help myself feel better. I developed a ritual for Sunday nights to deal with my anxiety. I would set my radio/alarm clock for thirty or forty minutes and lay back, listening to my favorite music at a subdued volume. As I listened I would imagine the worries that troubled my soul as a large ball—turbulent and dark—rising from my stomach up to God. As it rose out of my guts and toward "heaven," the music and imagery would soothe me. My body would release the tension I was carrying and I would soon drift off to sleep. I did not know then that I had stumbled onto a form of prayer—using the imagination to connect with God as the *Spiritual Exercises* of St. Ignatius Loyola prescribes. These early experiences of imagination and music prepped me for the spirituality I would embrace later as an adult.

Play On

Playing drums in a variety of bands for twenty years has been a valuable and treasured part of my life. My first "band" was comprised of myself and three of my siblings using Tupperware containers, tennis rackets, and cardboard paper towel rolls as makeshift instruments to perform an "air-band" version of Def Leppard's "Pyromania" to our very kind and understanding (but sorely confused) grandparents. By this time (early '80s), I knew that I loved rock music so I attempted guitar lessons for a couple of years. My interest in playing guitar eventually waned and my passions turned to the drums.

I credit Liberty DeVitto, Billy Joel's drummer for thirty years, for helping me fall in love with the drums. My interest in drumming did not come from being attracted to the instrument so much as it was being attracted to watching DeVitto mercilessly beating the instrument! DeVitto always played hard—he furiously pounded the drumheads as if they were threatening his life. I believe to this day that my attraction to playing the drums came from a desire within to externalize some angst that was building up inside of me. Some of this angst was due to normal hormone-driven teenage stuff, but some was also the result of feeling directionless and anxious and desiring to know what the hell I was meant to do with my life.

The angst and frustration certainly reflected in my playing style. During one practice with my first "real" band, the Stonemasons, I somehow put my drumstick through both the top *and* bottom heads of the snare drum. We would also receive regular complaints from the eighth floor of the University of Michigan residence hall where we practiced—even though we were in a ground level lounge! Playing drums during this time was, for me, an aerobic sport. Style, finesse, and technique were not of interest to me—I just wanted to hit something. I was learning about the physicality of rock music and the importance of the body in rock. As I became a better player, I believe that I became more comfortable with my body—not an easy task for a young adult male (or female) in a society that focused (and still does) so much attention on superficial beauty and ripped physiques. The first couple of years playing the drums allowed me to wildly express aggression in a socially acceptable way and begin to acquire the discipline of paying attention to my body's movements and limitations—and testing those limitations through my intense playing style.

Normally a subdued and laid-back guy, I noticed that I was different behind the drum kit—it was an "inhibition-free" zone. I played wildly, flashing crazy facial expressions and exhibiting an aggressive persona that rarely showed itself at other times. It was an experience of inner freedom, something that many people of faith pursue for a lifetime. This freedom did not envelop my entire life, but it was a refreshing oasis in the midst of anxiety, which seemed to be my constant companion as a young man. Behind the drums I was a playful character; I twirled my drumsticks and I even perfected a move where I toss my right stick in the air and catch it in time for the next snare drum beat. This behavior was not part of my "normal" life where I was responsible, serious, and mature. Trying to integrate more of the playful, even goofy, aspects of my personality into my "mainstream" life is a spiritual struggle that continues with me today, but it is an important and necessary one, and I would never have discovered it without my love for rock and drumming.

I have developed some very close and important friendships with some of my bandmates over the years. When I moved away from home for the first time to attend graduate school at Iowa State University, I became more serious about developing my drumming skills. I was lucky to meet Joe L., a fellow science grad student who became not only a great friend but is also one of the finest rock bass players I know. Joe and I have played together in several bands, and we developed a sense of each other's playing to the point where we could improvise in the middle of a song and hold a tight groove, until finally emerging into the chorus or bridge with stopwatch precision. This level of playing takes some skill and a lot of practice. But it also requires immense patience, something that Joe holds in abundance, and I am grateful to him for being patient with me and teaching me to be more patient with myself. Joe can tirelessly go over a troublesome part of a song until the whole band understands and can play it confidently.

In a band there has to be mutual respect and understanding, otherwise no negotiation or compromise can occur. There are good life lessons to learn, but even more important for me was learning about how to risk exposing my playful musician self to others and trust that it will be received generously. Joe and our mutual friend Bryon, the guitar player we rocked with in our band Sinema, helped me develop this much-needed gift over the years. We never made much of an impact outside of Ames, Iowa, but playing in this band was (and continues to be) one of the most important, formative aspects of my life. These two men have continued to be great friends to me for almost twenty years, and we reunite for gigs and recording every year or so to renew the friendship and make some music together.

One of the recent reunions occurred the day before my wedding in September of 2008. My then-fiancée Carrie and I had taken a lot of time to plan a meaningful Catholic wedding. We focused on the sacrament of matrimony being one of service—service to God, service to each other, and service to our fellow human beings. As a sign of the service we offered to each other, Carrie and I included a footwashing ceremony. After we exchanged vows, each of us took off our right shoe and we washed each other's foot. It was a simple sign to express our service, out of love, for each other. The night before the wedding, a reunited Sinema played a show at a local bar as a sign of love and service to all of our wedding guests. When I brought this idea up to Carrie, she enthusiastically agreed that it would be great to do something for our guests the night before, especially those who had traveled many miles to attend the wedding. It would also be the first time some of our guests had seen me play the drums.

It could seem to some that the notion of "service" was just an excuse to rock out before my wedding! I cannot deny that I had an absolute blast playing music with my friends in front of a packed house. But I sincerely desired this event to be of service to people I love and cherish. This is not, however, a unique idea. Playing the night before my wedding, perhaps, was unique, but the concept that rock music performance can be a form of service is something that I have witnessed numerous times by musicians who care for their fans. A number of my favorite rock musicians understand this—Springsteen, Rush, King's X, and many others. They know that playing music is not meant to be a self-focused activity. By its nature, music should be heard and appreciated. Music can also encourage virtue, especially in the musician. Practicing music as a form of service can build within a musician a foundation of caring and shift one's focus to the good of the other rather than oneself. For an example, I call upon one of the best drummers I have ever heard.

Bill Bruford is best known as the drummer for the progressive rock bands Yes, King Crimson, and U.K., although he also had a brief stint in Genesis. He recently wrote an autobiography to address some of the questions fans have asked him over the years. It is always fascinating to me to find out what goes on behind the scenes of a famous musician's life. More often than not, the reality is not as glamorous as I envision. One thing that struck me about Bruford's book was that he struggled with doubts about his playing, and also that other much younger players have intimidated him. These inner struggles, at times, led Bill to question why he remains a drummer. The answer that he developed over four decades of playing is masterful:

> Personally, I see music as a path to change. It works much like a mirror: music will show you your reflection, but if you don't much like what you see, you can change through music. You can become a different person through your striving, possibly a better person. Those of a religious nature would claim that right artistic endeavour could bring you closer, no matter how infinitely small the distance, to God. However bad you are today, honest application will

render you a better musician than you were yesterday. Musical endeavour offers a sense of progress.[2]

Bruford's words resonate with my own experience as an amateur musician, as well as my experience as a fan and audience member watching some rock musicians serving a crowd. Sometimes a rock show seems like much more than entertainment. Rock is such a somatic practice—utilizing the whole body and sometimes pushing it to extremes— and there are rockers who appear to be giving their entire selves to the audience. These are moments when, I believe, the rock musician exhibits a "forgetting of the self" and, in so doing, becomes to some extent a more other-focused individual. The performance moves from another mode of self-congratulatory narcissism toward becoming a self-gift to fellow human beings. Through this practice of self-giving, a musician can become better—not only as a musician but also as a human being.

Listening Room

I consider myself lucky to have developed some long-lasting friendships in my life. Three of my closest and oldest friends, Dan, Brian, and Jim, share with me an intense appreciation for rock music. The differences in taste between us are just great enough to have encouraged over

[2] Bill Bruford, *Bill Bruford: The Autobiography* (London: Jawbone Press, 2009), 141.

two decades of debates about rock music and how our personal preferences trump everyone else. Examples of topics that have stirred up the most heated exchanges include The Who vs. the Rolling Stones—which group is better? The Replacements—are they the best band of the 1980s? Finally, how many founding members of "classic rock" bands must still be in the lineup to legitimize the use of the original name? Just one of these questions has provided literally years of entertaining banter. We know just how to incite each other into a rabid, mouth-foaming verbal spar about rock and roll. In recent years, however, some of these interactions have become more formalized.

My friend Jim first had the idea. What would happen if we were to gather as a group of four once every couple of months and share some music that we love, all of it focused on a specific topic? The name we came up with for these gatherings is "the listening room." The topic, by the way, has since changed from decision by democratic vote to the easier, although more dictatorial, "host's choice." The format is simple: each man brings five songs to share, chosen to connect with the topic. After drawing numbers to determine the order in which we will play our selections, we begin and continue until all have played their selections. Some of these topics have included Best Guitarists to Have Emerged Since 1980, Guilty Pleasures, Best Songs You've Never Heard Of, Best Covers, Best Album Side. These occasions, which always include generous helpings of food and drink, have been exciting and enlightening, and they have served as great bonding experiences.

We all love rock music and we are all excited to play for each other the selections over which we have brooded for hours or days. There is also, I believe, something else going on here that is spiritually enriching and immensely important to the four of us.

There are few opportunities for men in U.S. society to share their passions, joys, and vulnerabilities with one another. It is not encouraged and many men are neither good at nor comfortable doing it. Father Richard Rohr, a Franciscan priest who has written and spoken extensively on male spirituality, has stated that female spirituality is more comfortable with the interior life and male spirituality is more comfortable with the exterior life. The exterior life manifests itself in performing actions rather than meditating and reflection, which are more interior activities.

I recall, when I was a Jesuit seminarian, the agonizing grimaces on not a few men's faces when we were mandated to do "faith sharing." This consisted in talking about what was going on in our lives and how it affected us—the dreaded interior life. How do we find God (or not) in current life events? What struggles are we facing for which we could use support? These opportunities were not always welcomed at the time, but now I grieve their loss. A balanced spirituality must hold both masculine and feminine aspects together, thus developing within a person some comfort with the exterior and interior aspects of oneself. There are few opportunities for men outside of the religious life to express those facets of their personhood that are typically hidden from view—namely, the interior, intimate and vulnerable aspects.

I believe that my three friends and I have stumbled on a method for men who love rock music to safely express their vulnerability with one another. This could seem strange to some since rock and roll, at least certain expressions of the culture and ethos, encourages the image of men as rebellious party animals with uncontrolled libidos. Such images, however, are incomplete—just slivers of more substantive and compelling aspects of masculinity (and rock music too, for that matter). A healthy masculine spirituality does not deny the desire for rebellion or the libido as part of what comprises a particular man's inner life. But it goes beyond these to a more holistic understanding of the complexity of humanity. When our group of four men shares rock music with each other, we are giving voice to facets of ourselves that are rarely revealed to other men. The format of our gatherings includes each man providing an explanation for why he chose the song he is about to play for the group. These introductions regularly expose our emotional ties, passions, and the memories we associate with the songs. Even if the connections are not that profound, the passion with which we describe some songs speaks volumes about its meaning and importance to our lives.

The emotional connection that some have with rock music is a theme brilliantly addressed in the film *High Fidelity*. John Cusack plays record store owner and music snob Rob Gordon. Rob has experienced one failed relationship after another and he is in the midst of the most recent ugly breakup when the film begins. Soon after his ex-girlfriend Laura moves out of their Chicago apartment,

Rob decides to rearrange his vinyl record collection. This act is a metaphor for attempting to put some order in the shambled mess that is his soul. Music is the only thing in Rob's life, other than women, about which he has shown any sense of uninhibited passion. When Laura leaves, Rob's inner life is a mess, so he turns in supplication to his other love for respite from the emotional hurricane he has just experienced. It is not uncommon for adults to find comfort in the rock music that has accompanied them and provided comfort at various times. In fact, there are many emotional ties that we can have with rock music and the role that particular songs played in our lives. I know that I use the listening room preparation as an opportunity to reflect on these ties.

When my friends and I are wandering through our record collections to find material to share with one another, this is an act similar to St. Ignatius's Examen prayer. This prayer encourages reflection on the past in order to locate where God has been active in one's life. Pouring through a record/CD collection can be an important method for getting in touch with the past, where we have found consolation or desolation in life events and for what we are most grateful. During these musical investigations, the memories and emotional energy contained within particular albums or songs necessarily find new space within my psyche as I sift through my music collection. Some songs have taken on completely new meanings in my late thirties that I could never have foreseen as a teenager when I first heard them. Other songs have continued to have the same grip on me and elicit laughter, tears, or melancholy as they did twenty-five years ago. When choosing songs for the listening room, I have passed on particular songs because I knew that playing them again would be much too emotionally wrenching. But as a rule, expressing how important certain songs are to us is encouraged and respected. I, for one, can testify to the spiritual enrichment I experience each time we meet.

The Real Me

In the summer of 1997 when I was a second-year novice in the Jesuits, my fellow novices and I embarked on an eight-day retreat on the campus of the University of Detroit Mercy. I recall two important highlights from this retreat. The first is that the Detroit Red Wings won the Stanley Cup on day five of the retreat! Perhaps my mind should have been on more spiritual pursuits, but I was thrilled for the team and the city. The other memorable part of the retreat came during a session with my spiritual director, a Jesuit priest named Mark. This session was so important to me because it initiated a more intentional connection between rock music and my spiritual life.

When I started this retreat, I was incredibly tense and exhausted. I had recently returned from a six-month assignment working at a retreat house just outside of Cincinnati. During this time, I worked with a great team of young adults giving retreats to high school students. One of the benefits of working with high school students is that they knew all about the music scene at the time. As a Jesuit novice attempting to live a vow of poverty, I had not been able to purchase many CDs, nor did I have much time to listen to the radio. The students, on the other hand, had plenty of time and disposable income, and carried dozens of CDs with them on these retreats. It was invigorating to talk about music with these students and hear about bands that were not part of my (then) limited cultural world. If a song was written after 1992, I probably did not know it. Now, with the help of some Catholic high school students, I was discovering new material by such bands as No Doubt, Live, Barenaked Ladies, and Guster. This was an invigorating exploration of new music and when my assignment was complete, I left for Detroit with a ton of new music to enjoy throughout the summer.

I always brought rock music to listen to on my retreats. Since these were supposed to be silent retreats, this may seem to be contradictory. But music was not forbidden, as long as we did not crank it and bother others. I always told my spiritual director that I was listening to music, and it was generally up to me to decide when listening crossed the line from a mode of relaxation to a means of avoiding issues on my heart that I did not want to face.

During my first spiritual direction meeting with Mark, I recall unloading all of my anxieties on him, telling him that something just did not feel "right" to me. After explaining how distraught I was feeling, Mark asked me if there was anything exciting or life-giving—anything for which I was thankful. I told Mark about all of the great new music that I was enjoying and how the teenagers on the various retreats had helped me find this joy. Mark recognized that the excitement with which I spoke about rock music seemed to be absent in the rest of my life. He suggested that I spend some time praying within that excitement and try to meet God there. Such a simple recommendation, but it forever altered the way that I approach my spiritual life.

Prior to this moment, I had never thought of my love of music as a spiritual exercise or a way to grow closer to God. Prayer is meant to be in silence, or perhaps with light Gregorian chant playing in the background. But Mark was suggesting that I dwell within the palpable excitement and passion that I feel when listening to rock music and meet God there. For the rest of the retreat I attempted this type of praying, but it was incredibly difficult. I could sense myself resisting, as if I was only willing to turn over certain parts of my life to God but not all of it. What would God do with my passion for music? I definitely did not want to start playing Christian rock or join a church folk group. Rock music was my soul's salve, my escape from anxiety— something that I loved for no other reason than because I loved it. Was I afraid that God would change me or my love for rock music, or begin using it for some greater purpose that I could not see? Whatever the reason, the resistance continued throughout the week, and it seemed as though I would never juxtapose these various aspects of my life and feel some peace.

On the final day of the retreat, about one hour before the closing mass, I took a walk and tried to pray. Once again I approached the notion that God wanted to meet me in my passion for rock music and once again I resisted. I began talking to God about it. I told God that I was not trying to be selfish, but I just couldn't give up my love for rock music and I did not want it to be utilized for some higher purpose. It was just something I loved. As I said these things to God, I was struck by my own words. Who had said anything about "giving up" rock music? Why had I phrased it in such a drastic way? My spiritual director Mark had simply recommended praying with my passion for music and meeting God there. I had interpreted that as giving up my passion to God. Why could it not just be a way to enjoy God's presence and gifts in my life rather than giving something up, or assuming that God wanted to take it away from me? This was a genuine spiritual experience—as soon as I realized what I had been doing, the anxiety and pressure poured out of me and I felt a lightness and joy about my life.

Ever since this experience, I have tried to incorporate my love for rock music and the joy I feel listening to it into my prayer. I listen to music and I revel in the euphoria I experience as a gift from God. A temptation for me is to close this aspect of my life off from prayer because of the fears I described previously. This just encourages a spiritual schizophrenia and does not acknowledge God's place in my entire life—not just in those things I had formerly deemed "holy."

Holy Cards

I've attended dozens of rock concerts in my life and I have saved ticket stubs for about 90 percent of them. These small paper souvenirs remind me of the holy cards that

Catholics cherish in their devotions to the saints or to a deceased loved one. Every ticket stub holds a bevy of memories, feelings, and desires for me—I need only pick one up, gaze at the date and venue, and I know exactly where I sat, who was with me, and any other unique details about the show. These cards are reminders of what I term "musical consolations." In his *Spiritual Exercises*, Ignatius Loyola recommends storing our moments of consolation from which we can draw during the inevitable desolation that will occur in all lives. These stubs are my musical consolations and I often return to them for comfort.

Recently, looking through my collection of ticket stubs, I came across one for an outdoor summer concert featuring Rush a couple of years ago. I brought my fiancée (now wife) Carrie to the show and I recall my desire for doing this was not because she is a huge fan (she has since grown in appreciation for Rush!) but because I wanted to show her something I loved dearly. The music and the experience of seeing a great rock band perform buoy my spirit. I wanted to show Carrie this part of me—perhaps it is a part that is not as well integrated as I would like, but it is an aspect of my personality that is full of energy, vigor, and passion. During the show, as is my usual practice, I was air-drumming, singing along to every song, and generally acting as one without inhibitions! After the show, as we waited for the crowd above us in the amphitheater to clear out, a couple fought their way against the crowd to come to us. They expressed amazement at how I was able to air-drum along with every song and they said they had as much fun watching me as the band. I am normally one who hates calling attention to himself, but I enjoyed listening to this couple recount what they saw in me.

Rock music can provide an avenue for sharing something that a person is unable to articulate through his or her own words. Carrie and I recently watched a documentary about Rush that covered the history of the band and included interviews with famous musicians who expressed how Rush had influenced them. Billy Corgan, guitarist and vocalist for The Smashing Pumpkins, was featured in a number of interview clips in the film. At one point Corgan is explaining how he was a very shy and quiet teenager and did not emote well. He recalls listening to Rush's song "Entre Nous" (between us) and feeling that it explained feelings within him that he did not have the vocabulary to express. He asked his mom to just sit and listen to the song with him because he desperately needed to reveal an aspect of himself but was unable to do it on his own. He did not even know what exactly he was trying to say, only that the song said it for him. The music, he believed, could be his emotional spokesperson.

It is easy for me to understand what Corgan was saying. There are moments of aesthetic pleasure that are, perhaps, only meant to be experienced and not talked about. How does one explain seeing a breathtaking piece of artwork or being in the room when your wife gives birth to your first child? Our limited vocabularies cannot do justice to the experience. Corgan's desire to have his mother just sit and listen with him came out of an ache he had to connect, but he realized that the connection could not be built by his own feeble attempts. He needed something more transcendent. This is what I was attempting to do with Carrie—I was trying to reveal something about myself that I felt inadequate doing with my own words. Is it odd or silly for me to believe that God was present at that rock show, enabling me to reveal part of my soul to another and build a stronger connection through my interaction with the music?

Talkin' 'bout the Next Generation

As the father of an infant son, I wonder about his future and, specifically, what role music will play in his life. I do not want to thrust my personal tastes upon him, but I hope to encourage within him a love for music. Rock music has been an important part of my life for several years. It is my comfort from anxiety, it has helped me build several friendships, it has provided me with emotional outlets and release when I needed it most, and it has accompanied me through some of the most difficult and joyous phases of my life. I hope my son experiences some of these gifts that rock music has offered in my life and the lives of many others.

As my wife and I teach our son about religious faith and the important role our faith has held through our lives, I will tell him about the connection between my faith and my love for rock music. I want to encourage him to not place limitations on God and how God can work in his life. And if one day he asks me to accompany him to a club or auditorium to see a rock show, I cannot pretend that I will not be thrilled by the opportunity to connect with him in this special way and watch his face beam when the "holy trinity" of guitar, bass, and drums explodes onstage. Perhaps he will experience, as I have, how rock music can help someone grow into an authentic, integrated, spiritual person.

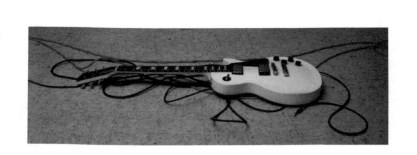